Endorseme

For many years it h .... ,, ...,
to publish a book of her writings. She has always been wonderful
at bringing a simple story to life in the telling, or in this case
the writing. A woman of strong faith and unconditional love for
family and friends, she has taken some everyday life experiences
and, together with biblical instructions, created easily understood picture stories that help one honor our Lord and Savior,
Jesus Christ, and find joy in the little unexpected happenings
of our lives. I love the way she is an example to me and many
others of the woman in Proverbs 31, where it says, "She looks
well to the ways of her household and her children will rise up
and call her blessed." For sure, Mom has been this wonderful
woman for her children, grandchildren, and great-grandchildren, and we all look forward to many more years of experi-
encing the warmth of her love, be it in a hug or a great story
told or written, sitting at her kitchen table. Love you, Mom.

—Mona Lea

In 2 Timothy 1:5 Paul wrote to Timothy, his disciple, of
Timothy's genuine faith in Jesus Christ as Savior. He mentions
that his genuine faith dwelt first in his grandmother, then his
mother, and now in him! I think that I will have to claim the
same. I first learned of Jesus Christ at my mother's side. Every
step of life was bathed in the light of knowing Christ. Mom
was always teaching my siblings and me about Jesus and about
the right choices of the Christian life. I certainly didn't follow
them like I should have, but it was because I did not come to
Christ until I was fifteen. I must say, though, that my con-
sciousness of God came primarily from my mother, who laid a

foundation to help me know that I needed the grace and mercy and forgiveness and love of God through the gift of His Son, Jesus Christ. I could not earn it by good works (since I didn't have any, anyway!).

I trust that the light of my mother's meditations written at her kitchen table will enlighten you more about the love of Jesus. I always picture her sitting at her kitchen table praying to her Lord or writing something from her heart to share with the world about her personal Lord. You can believe Jesus is real to my mom, Jean Susan Rudolph! Love you, Mom.

—Ken

Jean Susan Klotzbach Rudolph is my mom. She has always been a great storyteller and great at creative writing. She wrote poems for each of her four children, and within each poem is a story. My mom was a Sunday school teacher from the age of fourteen to the age of eighty-five. I had the privilege of being one of those many children she touched with her faith. A true blessing to me is that my children and the three oldest of my grandchildren also witnessed her love for Jesus and her love for teaching Sunday school. A story comes to life when Mom creates the event in words. Her faith is strong, and she is loving to all. My parents' kitchen table is always open to anyone who is hungry or thirsty for their comfort and their encouragement. I have been blessed with wonderful God-loving parents, and I'm so happy Mom is having her dream come true in writing these devotionals for all to read.

Love you so much,
Your daughter, Betty

"Great is the LORD, and greatly to be praised; and His greatness is unsearchable. One generation shall praise Your works to another, and shall declare Your mighty acts" (Ps. 145:3–4, NKJV). I can remember my mom reading to me from the children's Bible at bedtime. She is a great storyteller and would bring those stories to life. My grandfather was a preacher and handed down this gift of conveying God's insight from one generation to the next.

The kitchen table is the heart of our home, overlooking farm fields and woods, where Mom sits at the same seat at the table next to my dad. It is always a place of love, laughter, and fellowship. This is the place where God inspires her writings.

Scripture is linked to our salvation, and many times we hear that in a sermon, but my mom lives it. She is an example of godliness, caring for and showing the love of Jesus to others selflessly and with joy.

Her stories of love and faith reach, encourage, and inspire. I am honored to hear from others that my mom has blessed them with the insight of God.

—Tracy Rudolph, Jean's youngest son.

At My
KITCHEN
TABLE

Psalms 34:8 "Oh, taste and see that the Lord is good; blessed is the one who takes refuge in Him."

Jean S. Rudolph

XULON PRESS

Xulon Press
2301 Lucien Way #415
Maitland, FL 32751
407.339.4217
www.xulonpress.com

Paperback ISBN-13: 978-1-6628-1791-5

Ebook ISBN-13: 978-1-6628-1792-2

Dedication:

To my husband, Richard.

THANKS FOR BEING MY HUSBAND AND LOVING ME unconditionally for these past seventy-two years, and for putting up with me during those times when I was not so lovable. Thanks for becoming the spiritual leader in our home and for being a great father to our four children. Thanks also for your strength and fortitude in providing for your family and for your devotion in serving Jesus. Colossians 3:23: "Whatever you do, work at it with all your heart, as working for the Lord, not for men." (NIV)

Contents

Acknowledgments:

To my husband, Richard, for his encouragement in getting these meditations into a book, and to my four children: Mona for all her work in putting these devotions in order; Kenneth and his wife, Jinner, for their loving support; Betty and her husband, David "Boots" Hall, for believing in my book; Tracy and his wife, Laurie, who pushed me into action.

To relatives, friends, neighbors, loved ones, and people I didn't even know for telling me how much they enjoyed my articles, printed in the *Daily News* in Batavia, New York. A big thank you to those who wrote me letters and notes through the mail and to those who did it on Facebook and via email; all this was appreciated and encouraging.

To my dad and mom, Peter and Clara Klotzbach, for raising me to love God and serve Him in whatever way I could, and I'm privileged to do that with my book, *At My Kitchen Table*. I hope those who read it will be encouraged in their spiritual life and that Jesus will become as real to them as He is to me.

Jean and Richard with their four children

Introduction:

WHEN I MARRIED RICHARD M. RUDOLPH, ON October 22, 1948, I was a young, happy bride of eighteen years of age. Life was great, and I was embarking on the new adventure of being a housewife. I was leaving my home in Indian Falls, New York, and moving into a brand-new house twenty miles away in Bennington, New York, up the road from Richard's parents' old farmhouse, where Richard was raised. We've moved four times since that day and now reside in a beautiful brick home on Akron Road in the same rural area, near where I was born.

Since that day seventy-two years ago, my life has been full of blessings, joys, and a few heartaches, but with Jesus as a third partner in our marriage, we have enjoyed the journey. As the years flew by, four children—Mona, Kenneth, Betty, and Tracy—were welcomed into the family. Today we now have four grown children, ten grandchildren, and twenty-six great-grandchildren, plus in-law children and in-law grandchildren—all of which makes us a family of fifty-six. Little did I realize that God would bless us so richly.

During those many years I have written poems, devotions, meditations for church programs, Christmas plays, and stories for my own pleasure. Then in July 2016, I started to write letters to the editor of our local newspaper in Batavia, New York. I titled my meditations "At My Kitchen Table," and he published them. It was a joy for me to see them in print, and it made me feel good when people told me how much they liked them. It's been my dream to have them put into a book through which I may tell others about my faith in God. Thanks to the encouragement of my husband and children, my dream is finally coming to life. I do hope you will enjoy the many stories and meditations as you read my book, *At My Kitchen Table*.

Jean and Richard

Letter #1
Writing from My Kitchen Table

July 1, 2016

AFTER READING YOUR DAILY NEWS AND SEVERAL of the articles, which I really enjoy, I decided that I needed to write you a letter. Paul Trowbridge, who writes articles from his "View from the Tractor Seat," is wonderful, easy to read, and down-to-earth about his farm and family. I also enjoy Tom Valley, who writes for the *Daily News*, always quite humorous and definitely informative, about his life and some of his troubles. That got me to thinking that maybe I should write articles called "At My Kitchen Table," as that is where I spend a good share of my time, and they would be from a woman's point of view.

Actually my kitchen table is also my dining room table, as my kitchen and dining room comprise one large space. But the kitchen is the room where I spend most of my time. I'm retired, up in age (eighty-five), married, and happy but still a housewife, which means I have all the chores do to that I did years ago when I first got married. Except I was younger, and I could do all those jobs faster, such as cleaning, preparing meals, washing clothes, and taking care of the kids. Now I still do them but slower, perhaps not as well, so they take more time to accomplish. You don't get much rest when you are puttering around in the kitchen getting three meals a day, cleaning the house, and washing the clothes. Not that I'm complaining, as I'm thankful that the good Lord has let me live this long and also that I have had a loving husband to care for these past sixty-seven years. In the Bible, in Proverbs 31:27–28, it says, "She watches over the affairs of her household and does not eat the bread of idleness. Her children arise and call her blessed; her husband also, and he praises her" (NIV).

So my kitchen table is a very important place for me. That is where my husband, Richard, and I enjoy breakfast and have our daily devotions every morning. That is also where I enjoy my coffee break later and watch the wildlife and beauty from my kitchen window. Sometime there are deer grazing in the farmer's field behind our house or bunnies, squirrels, and chipmunks running around. And if someone comes to visit, the kitchen table is available for a cup of coffee, a cookie or two, and friendly conversation. There is really no other place I'd rather be than at home at my kitchen table—eating, visiting, drinking coffee, playing games with my grandchildren, or watching God's beautiful world right outside my kitchen window.

I can also watch television from my kitchen table or read a book and even pray. I wish everyone were as blessed as I am—content, happy, loved, cherished, and with a kitchen table to enjoy. Thank you, Lord, for your grace and love; that's what makes a house a home. Guess that's all for today, from my kitchen table.

Letter #2

Another View from My Kitchen Table

July 16, 2016

I'M ALL ALONE, AND FOR ME IT'S A QUIET TIME—A time for prayer and a special time to read from my Bible. It's a beautiful day; the sun is shining as usual, and the temperature outside is already a warm 86 degrees. I'm cool inside with a 72-degree thermometer reading, thanks to a small air-conditioner placed in my kitchen window. It doesn't block my view, and it keeps me comfortable.

Actually there is a small problem that has interrupted my quiet time, and that is the steady drip-drip-drip coming from my kitchen faucet. It's not too disturbing but sort of annoying. My husband, Richard, has called the plumber, as that faucet is not on his list of things to do. Of course I'm saving every single drip in a dish, as I don't want to waste precious water. We haven't had enough rain this summer to keep our lawn green, so I certainly want to save on water, as we only have a well for our water supply. Our well has never run out, but one can never be too careful. I guess the habit of saving and being frugal was taught to me from little up, so it's just in my nature to save and not waste. Of course Richard told the plumber, Ken, not to hurry, as it was no big deal, and to come when he gets over our way. That's all right with me, as good plumbers are always busy. I can be patient as long as I know that someday soon it will be good as new.

There is a verse in the Bible, believe it or not, that talks about a constant dripping; it is found in Proverbs 19:13b: "And a quarrelsome wife is like a constant dripping." (NIV) Funny how something such as a dripping faucet can bring a certain verse to mind. A little reminder for me not to complain and to remember how annoying a quarrelsome wife or husband can be. As one gets older, like me, we have lots of things to complain about—all the aches and pains that seem to creep up on us, and before we know it, we are that constant drip-drip-drip. Guess I'm glad to have had that leaky faucet just to remind me to look at the brighter side of life. I'm still alive, still happy, still walking (with effort), able to take nourishment, and enjoying my family and friends. What more could one ask for than that?

Well, Ken came, that faucet has been fixed, and all is quiet once again. My kitchen table is a great place to gain a little wisdom by taking the time to meditate and enjoy some time alone. So pour yourself another cup of coffee, grab a couple cookies, and enjoy another view from my kitchen table.

Letter #3

Avoid Cluttering Your Life with Stuff

August 8, 2016

WELL, A LOT HAS HAPPENED SINCE THAT LAST VIEW from my kitchen table. I can't begin to tell you in one short letter but will try. A dear friend of mine has had to make the decision to leave her home and move to live with her daughter. She is too ill to do this by herself, so her son and daughter came from out of state and out of the country to help her. With little time to devote to this task, as they both have professions and families to get back to, they didn't know where to begin. For my friend, Marion, this means getting rid of her treasures, but to her family it's disposing of a lot of stuff that is no longer needed.

Looking around my kitchen and dining room, I can see many treasures that I have on display and want to keep, things that mean a lot to me. But when I'm forced to get rid of all this, who will really want my treasures? That lovely crystal vase I got from my great-niece for my sixtieth anniversary is something I treasure, but I'm sure it won't mean very much to my children. As I gaze around the rooms and see the china cabinet and the old antique secretary desk and other treasures, I too realize that I have a lot of "stuff."

I notice my Bible on the chair beside the table, and it brings to mind the question, "Do I have stuff I'm keeping that is cluttering up my life?" I don't mean just material things; I'm talking about stuff that is cluttering up my life in other ways, such as watching too much TV or being too busy and not taking time to pray. How about those angry words I said and forgot to say I was sorry? And what about not forgiving others but expecting God to forgive me? Am I holding on to resentment? Am I complaining? Am I letting envy and jealousy creep into my thoughts when I should be praising God for the many blessings He gives me every day? Yes, all that every day "stuff" that creeps ever so slowly into our lives and clutters up our days. I'm afraid I need to be on my guard and let God be in control so that I won't have stuff in my life that is useless. Matthew 6:19–21 says, "Do not store up for yourselves treasures on earth, where moth and rust destroy, and where thieves break in and steal. But store up for yourselves treasures in heaven, where moth and rust do not destroy, and where thieves do not break in and steal. For where your treasure is, there your heart will be also." (NIV)

My friend has moved, and her treasures are on their way to her new home. As I walked through the empty rooms, I was again reminded that all those material things we hold onto are actually just stuff. The true meaning of what we treasure is the life we have lived, those family members who love us, and the love of Jesus, who has made us who we are. The only treasure worth saving will be the love we hold in our hearts.

It was sad to see those empty rooms and know that I may never see my friend again. Yet I can treasure the memories and the good times we had when we were young. So I'll sit here at my kitchen table, have my second cup of coffee, and enjoy my stuff and the memories that go with it.

Letter #4

Watching the Harvest from My Kitchen Table

August 26, 2016

SEVERAL WEEKS AGO I WAS GAZING OUT THE window when the farmer from next door, Bill, began to harvest his oat crop. The field of oats is connected behind our one acre of land to the south, and his other fields surround us. What a joy to be able to live in the country and watch Bill as he works in his fields and observe his steers and horses across the road to the north. He is a great farmer, and we have enjoyed watching his crops grow the fifty-some years we have lived here. But this year, with the loss of rain and the drought conditions, those precious crops that produce food have not been so great. The oats, as they grow from those small seeds, are usually a green, shimmering color when they are first seen in the early part of June, and they grow tall and full to about a foot and a half. Not this year. The color was a dull brownish-green, and when they began to ripen and turn color, which is usually a golden yellow, it was sad to watch the growth stop at about a foot high and see the brownish-yellow color of the oats in those eight acres of land.

When Bill began to harvest that small field of oats on August 4, he pulled his large combine and wagons into the field, as he was the only one doing the work. Now back in my day, when I was a kid in the 1930s, at harvest time there would be several men working to harvest that field, and it would have taken all day to do the job. But Bill harvested those oats all in one afternoon. The crop of oats only ran sixty bushels to the acre, and he harvested only one hundred bales of straw. In a normal harvest, he would have had twice those amounts. Yes, Bill's harvest this year was only half a crop due to the lack of rain but was still worth the work for the food it provided for his animals.

This made me think about a verse in the Bible about harvesting. It's found in Matthew 9:37 (NIV) when Jesus is talking to His disciples and says, "The harvest is plentiful but the workers are few." Now, Jesus wasn't talking about food; He was talking about people. The plentiful harvest is the people of the world who do not know about the love of Jesus, and they are the fields that are ripe for harvest. The workers, the ones to tell others about Jesus' love, are few in number. I would like to be one of those workers and let others know about the Lord Jesus and His love for all people. I can't go into the world, but as I sit at my kitchen table, I can let others know the things I see that make me think of spiritual blessings. Life has so much to offer if we take a spiritual walk with Jesus each day and take time to pray. What a blessing for me to watch the harvesting of oats and compare it to Jesus, who wants to be the Harvester of my life and give me the riches of heaven.

Two mornings ago, once again Bill was out working in that empty field that was ragged and not looking too good. This time he was preparing it for another crop. First, he plowed the field with a five-bottom plow and then fitted the ground with what they call a cultimulcher machine. Next, he used a machine that spreads fertilizer over the soil, then another run with the cultimulcher machine, and the soil was ready for the new crop, all within one short afternoon. This is like life when we get rid of the old weeds of sin and let Jesus work in the soil of our hearts for new life with Him. It takes a lot of work, just like farming does. Praise God for hardworking farmers, who provide food for all of us. I'm happy to live where I do and have this special place at my kitchen table to enjoy life and share my thoughts with all of you.

Letter #5

View of the Highway from My Kitchen Table

September 9, 2016

WE WERE COMING BACK FROM BATAVIA AFTER shopping, and as we neared the construction of the new bridge going up on Route 5, near Bushville, my husband began to get excited, wondering how near to completion it might be. Then he noticed that we didn't have to stop for a red light or signs, as traffic was moving right along. I could hear the excitement in his voice as his eyes scanned the construction site and he exclaimed, "Look, Jean, it's done, and what a great job! It's beautiful, and they finished it before Labor Day weekend."

I too noticed, but I didn't have the appreciation he did. You see, my husband, Richard, was a superintendent of highways for thirty-two years, and he still gets a thrill out of road construction, new highways, the smell of blacktop, and all kinds of work on the roads wherever we travel. You've heard the saying that you can take the boy out of the farm, but you can't take the farm out of the boy; well, I guess that would be true about the road workers as well. You can retire from being a superintendent of highways, but you can never take the joy of building roads and plowing snow from a truly dedicated man who loved his job.

Another job Richard loved was farming; as a kid he worked on his dad's farm, before buying one of his own in the town of Pembroke in 1953. He was happy milking cows and farming the one hundred acres we owned, but when he became superintendent of highways in 1955, he tried to combine both jobs and found that his body didn't tolerate so much stress, so we sold the farm. Loving your job or occupation can make for one happy person, and that is what has happened in our household. He's ninety-one now and still loves to watch road construction, talk with other road workers, and relive the times he too worked in that capacity.

Speaking of roads reminds me of the highways I travel in this life. The highways, which are broad and filled with cars and trucks, can be dangerous. There are pot holes to dodge, other drivers to contend with, and road construction hazards, and if we don't travel with caution and obey the rules, it can be dangerous. That's also true in life. There is a verse in Matthew 7:13 that reminds us to obey the rules. It says, "Enter through the narrow gate. For wide is the gate and broad is the road that leads to destruction, and many enter through it. But small is the gate and narrow the road that leads to life and only a few find it." (NIV)

It's a joy for me to know that the narrow road I'm traveling in this life is the best way. When we travel that narrow road with Jesus in this life, we have a Driver with a steady hand helping us to navigate the highways here below. Traveling with Jesus on the narrow road is the safe way if we follow the rules. Traveling the broad way, we are on our own. The pot holes in life need to be dodged, and what better way than to travel with

Jesus, who can give us a safe journey to heaven. According to Revelation 21:21b, "The streets [in heaven] will be pure gold like transparent glass."(NIV) And I definitely want to see those golden highways. So I'll travel with Jesus on that narrow road that leads to eternal life and be thankful.

Yes, the bridge on Route 5 is completed, beautiful, and well-constructed. Of course there is still much work to be done before the entire project is finished, but for now the bridge is done, and I'm thankful for that. So as I travel this highway of life, I will make sure that the bridges I cross and the roads I travel are well constructed by the Master Builder until the entire project is finished and I'm safe at home in heaven with those streets of gold.

And that's the view from my kitchen table this Labor Day weekend.

Letter #6

Cleaning Up with Soap and the Bible

September 29, 2016

WELL, SUMMER IS WINDING DOWN. HOW DO I know? I just finished cleaning the outside grill. I'd been dreading the task. Every time I saw it as I walked by or drove out the driveway, there it was—that dirty, greasy monster waiting to be scrubbed. Our children bought the grill for us, as they thought we needed one, so we graciously accepted it but never used it for ourselves—only when we hosted picnics. My husband had been the one to use it. Not because he wanted to or liked to cook, but I do the cooking inside, and at my age, I was not going to start grilling outside. I think we only used it three or four times this summer, but today was the day to clean it up and put it away for the winter.

It took me about an hour-plus to clean and scrub off the grease and dirt before I was satisfied. Obviously, I then had to clean myself up; my apron had telltale signs of black grease, as did my shoes and hands. Of course I didn't put rubber gloves on before I started; that never entered my mind. I wasn't careful while scrubbing with the wire brush, so my shoes and apron were the results of my carelessness. Now as I scrubbed my hands with soap and a scrub brush, I realized they weren't coming clean. That black grease had penetrated my knuckles and under my fingernails and would not come clean. So I grabbed my Clorox to bleach out the dirt under my nails, to no avail. Now what to do? Then I had a great idea. Get that old bar of Fels-Naphtha soap out of the cupboard and see if that would work; that's known for getting rid of stains. So with a scrub brush, Fels-Naphtha soap, and a little elbow grease, once again the grit under my nails and in the creases of my knuckles was gone.

Sort of reminds me that life is like that. I let some black thoughts of sin and messy, dirty issues creep into my mind and heart, and before you know it, I need some cleaning up. A quick trip to my Bible, where I read this scripture in Psalm 51:1–2: "Have mercy on me, O God, according to your unfailing love; according to your great compassion blot out my transgressions. Wash away all my iniquity and cleanse me from my sin."(NIV) Wow, what a promise! Just as I washed my hands with good Ole Fels-Naphtha soap and got rid of the grease and dirt, so too I can go to my Heavenly Father and ask for forgiveness, and He will wash away all the black, dirty sin from my heart. Asking God to cleanse me from sin and praying for forgiveness will change my heart and give me a new love of life. God's solution for sin is His forgiveness, and that is a tried-and-true way that works every time. The old remedies are the best and are proven to get the job done in a hurry. Prayer and Bible reading are both great remedies for cleaning up one's life, just like Fels-Naphtha soap did for my hands.

It feels good knowing that the grill is clean, my hands are clean, and I've even asked God to clean up my life. I guess I'm ready to have that cup of coffee and sit back and enjoy the view from my kitchen table.

Letter #7
Family Reunion Brings Back Memories

October 13, 2016

WE HAD A GREAT TIME THIS PAST WEEKEND AROUND my kitchen table, as my baby sister, Ellen Carey, flew in from Arizona to attend our Peter Klotzbach Jr. family reunion at my brother's farm. The reunion has been held at this time of year for the last twenty years or so because of the fall season and the colorful beauty of God's handiwork. Years ago we use to have the reunion around my dad's birthday, which is on November 19, but my brother Milton, who lived in California, asked if we'd have it earlier, as he loved to see the panorama of the fall colors, which were much prettier than the dark and dreary colors of November. Also, if we had it on the Columbus Day weekend, the kids would be out of school and some of the adults would also have a holiday weekend from their work schedule and be able to travel. And it has worked out very well for many years.

So my sister Ellen, who is number thirteen of our family, flew here, and I was honored to have her stay at my home. Needless to say we had a great time as we spent some of her time here at my kitchen table. It was like old times reminiscing about by gone days, having a cup of coffee and just relaxing around my kitchen table. What fun we had as we recounted some of those days of yester year with some laughter and, yes, even some tears.

I said earlier that Ellen was number thirteen in our large family, so maybe I should catch you up on that part of my story. Ellen has written a book titled *A Baker's Dozen*, and the stories in that book tell about how my mom and dad raised their family of thirteen children with a great faith in God and lots of hard work and love. My mom and dad were given a large dining room table from my mom's father and mother as a wedding gift. Her father said to her, "Clara, this table will seat twelve; fill it up with grand-children." And that is what they did. I had six brothers and six sisters, of which I'm number ten in the lineup, but only four of us girls remain: Eleanor Kreutter, Kathryn Thurber, Ellen, and me.

I'm happy Ellen wrote that book, as it tells about the importance of my parents' faith and how they handed down that faith to us. The reading of the Bible and having prayer time every day was number one for them, and we kids were included in that daily devotional time. No matter what we were doing or where we were going, that came first, and so did their love of God. In Deuteronomy 11:18–19, God says, "Fix these words of mine in your hearts and minds; tie them as symbols on your hands and bind them on your foreheads. Teach them to your children, talking about them when you sit at home and when you walk along the road, when you lie down and when you get up." (NIV) And that is what my parents did: they lived their faith and showed that faith of God to us. Now we in turn have to pass that faith on to others.

My three sisters and I had a great time at the reunion as we greeted brothers-in-law, sisters-in-law, nephews, nieces, and their offspring during the delicious chicken barbecue, which was furnished by the Harry Klotzbach family along with many other dishes that were brought by family members. About eighty-five attended, but it could have been well over two hundred or more. It was a day to remember, and I'm sure we will do just that, as many pictures were taken.

As we sat around my kitchen table for the last time, before Ellen returned home, there was much laughter and a few tears before we took her to the airport. But there was also that feeling of love—that no matter how far away we would be from each other, we would have the memories of the love and faith our parents handed down to us around that kitchen table so many years ago. And that is why the "view from my kitchen table" gives me such joy as I share that view with all of you.

Peter Klotzbach Jr. Family 1940 (Jean to Left with bow in her hair)

Letter #8

Fall Season's Beauty Causes Reflection

November 7, 2016

TODAY AS I'M SITTING AT MY KITCHEN TABLE drinking my second cup of coffee and enjoying the view, I observe the fall and seasonal decorations my daughter Mona has arranged all around the kitchen, dining room, and in the living room. She's done a great job with all those colors—oranges, yellows, browns, greens, and brick reds. There are flowers, small ears of yellow and brown corn, pilgrims, turkeys, pumpkins, and scarecrows, all beautifully arranged with a welcome sign in the middle proclaiming, AUTUMN HAS ARRIVED. The rooms are filled with the colors that shout, "Be happy, be joyful, and enjoy the beauty of the colors and decorations that shout hello. I'm that special season of fall, and I'm here."

Actually the view today from my kitchen window is beautiful; the sun is shining, and the fall colors are in full array outside with the same colors that Mona decorated my rooms. The leaves that have fallen cover the lawn in a blanket of magnificent colors painted by God, and as a gentle breeze tumbles them to and fro, they look like they're dancing. I'm also keeping in mind that soon they will need to be raked and cleared away. Actually God's handiwork this fall has been exceptional, and the weather has been quite warm for this time of the year.

When my daughter Mona was born in November years ago, it was rather cold and nippy as we traveled to the hospital, but today it is 60 degrees. So how can I not be cheerful when God provides us with so many blessings? With eyes to see all the beauty of this fall season of the year, I truly have a lot to be thankful for, which brings to mind that Thanksgiving Day is almost here. A special day set aside to remember to give thanks for all we have.

Let me ask you, "Do you really celebrate that day with the giving of thanks, or do you only look forward to that feast of turkey, dressing, and pumpkin pie, to the football game and a quick nap afterward? In Psalm 100:4 it says, "Enter his gates with thanksgiving and his courts with praise; give thanks to him and praise his name." (NIV) Now, that is a great idea to enter into His presence with thanks and praise, and it's not hard to do either. Giving thanks for all He's done for me in exchange for His love and grace—it's a no-brainer. Looking at the colors of His handiwork, the great weather, beautiful sunsets, good health, this great country I live in, and my family and friends that I love and enjoy, I have much to be thankful for. So this Thanksgiving on November 24, I plan on taking a few moments to bow my head and give thanks to Him for everything. And maybe, just maybe, I'll do that as I sit at my kitchen table before my Thanksgiving Day turkey dinner.

Letter #9

Reminded of the Biggest Gift This Season

November 25, 2016

IT'S THE DAY AFTER THANKSGIVING, AND I'M SITting at my kitchen table enjoying the solitude and quiet after a blessed, wonderful Thanksgiving Day with family and friends. It is a little overcast and the temperature outside is 42 degrees—a typical fall day here in western New York. It's not raining now, but earlier this morning there were a few sprinkles. But nothing is going to dampen my spirits this day, as yesterday was such a great time with family and friends. Not all the family came, as many of them live out of state, but still thirteen of them came for a great feast that everyone helped to provide, which made it easier for my husband and me to host, so today I'm relaxing.

No, I'm not celebrating Black Friday, as my legs and feet are not good enough to tolerate the standing and walking that shopping entails. Actually I have everything I need, so no reason to join the hassle of shoving and pushing that Black

Friday seems to entail. And getting up early to stand in line to get those deals doesn't thrill me. But for my daughter Betty and her daughter Teri, that's another story! On Thanksgiving Day after dinner, they pored over all the advertisements we received in the Wednesday edition of the *Daily News*, and there were a lot of ads. They began searching and looking forward to the thrill of Black Friday, which started on Thanksgiving night at 6:00 p.m. Christmas is coming, and the challenge of reduced prices and all those great bargains started Betty and Teri planning to take advantage of all those wonderful sales on Black Friday.

Oh, to be young again and enjoy the thrill of shopping for Christmas gifts. Yes, I used to love shopping for my four children and ten grandchildren, but when the great-grandchildren came along, it got to be too much, and with the wrapping of the gifts, it was no longer fun but a lot of work. Besides, half of them lived out of state, with families of their own, and they no longer came home at Christmastime. So I took the easy way out, and I now give money. No gifts to wrap, no packages to send, and I can still look forward to the giving of a gift, even though it is only money. Kids and grown-ups like getting those twenty-dollar bills in their Christmas stockings, and best of all, we love giving them. It's not much, but it shows that we love them.

God too loves to give His children good gifts, so He lovingly sent the gift of His Son, Jesus. In John 3:16 it says, "That God so loved the world, that He gave his only Son, [Jesus], that whosoever believeth in him shall not perish, but have everlasting life."(KJV) That gift of Jesus was given to us many years ago, for free. All we have to do is accept that gift. We don't have to look for a bargain, as He is already a bargain at no cost to us. He's not a Black Friday deal; He's a deal available every day. So as I sit at my kitchen table, I'm again reminded to be thankful for all of His blessings to me and most of all to be thankful that I have Him as my Savior. And I'm also thankful that I'm sitting here enjoying my second cup of coffee and not out shopping on this special Black Friday.

Letter #10

Early Christmas Gift

December 9, 2016

WELL, I'M NOT SITTING AT MY KITCHEN TABLE AS much, as I've been busy on the Internet and on Facebook keeping in touch with relatives in Virginia. My granddaughter Julie and her husband, Andrew, welcomed a tiny early Christmas present, and I do mean early and very tiny. This gift was expected to arrive in January, but for some reason she decided to come early, amid a lot of hurrying of doctors, nurses, and family. Dad arrived in time to see her arrival during an emergency C-section birth, and then little Emily was rushed away to an incubator, as she weighted only two pounds, six ounces.

Her Grandma Laurie and Grandpa Tracy here in western New York hurriedly called to let us all know and to tell us to please be in prayer for them, as it was a grave situation. I began phoning everyone I knew to ask them to start praying, as I wanted God to be there with them in Virginia and wanted Him to know how much we needed His saving touch on Julie and Emily's lives. And God answered our prayers as we all interceded, asking for God's help in healing and taking charge of this whole situation. Prayer is a valuable tool to reach God, and it works.

Little Emily Grace is now doing well but still needs our prayers. Julie too is out of danger, and it's only been a little more than a week. But what a week it was! Of course the grandparents from up here in New York traveled down to be there for a few days, and they kept us informed by Facebook and phone of all that was going on. And best of all, they sent pictures so that we could see that tiny little angel; it was almost like being there. I've copied several of the pictures of her mom and dad as they looked into the incubator, and they are precious pictures I wouldn't have if I didn't have Facebook.

That got me to thinking of that first Christmas night when Mary and Joseph arrived in Bethlehem, and they didn't have a place to stay. Mary was about to give birth, with no doctor or nurses present to help with the delivery—only Joseph. The Bible gives the only account of what happened that night, and that is told in Luke 2:7, which says, "And she brought forth her first born son, and wrapped him in swaddling clothes, and laid him in a manger; because there was no room for them in the Inn."(KJV) This gift was perfect—the perfect size in every way. No incubator, just a manger filled with hay. And now a precious baby boy lay there, with angels proclaiming His birth. No phones or internet to tell the good news, only some lowly shepherds who came to worship Him, and they left to proclaim the good news to others.

The birth of Emily came at a time when we were not expecting her, and I think Jesus came at a time when the people in Bible times weren't expecting Him either. Only God knew the time for Emily to be born, and He also knew the perfect time to send Jesus, His only son. Only Mary knew that this was

God's son, and in Luke 2:19 it says, "But Mary kept all these things, and pondered them in her heart."(KJV)

Jesus was born in a lowly stable with angels and a star to proclaim the good news. Emily was born in a state-of-the-art hospital and was attended by doctors and nurses, with people logged in from far and wide to see this beautiful little girl through the miracle of Facebook. Yes, we love little Emily without really seeing her or touching her, and that is the way we feel about Jesus, who was born in a manger so long ago. We haven't actually seen Him or touched Him, but He is real, and it's God's gift to us. I've received that gift of Jesus into my heart, and it was the best gift that God could give.

So forgive me for sitting at my computer, as I don't want to miss a single Facebook message about this precious, tiny little girl. And if you don't want to miss the message of Jesus, be sure to read the story in your Bible found in Luke 2:1–20, and you can also visit any church in the area on any Sunday, and they'll be happy to help you celebrate Jesus' birthday. Now let me wish you a Merry Christmas, everyone, and as always, it's from my kitchen table.

Letter #11
The Old Is Gone, the New Has Come
December 31, 2016

I'M SITTING AT MY KITCHEN TABLE READING THE *Daily News* and enjoying a little timeout. I'm reading a day-old *Daily News* that I was too busy to read earlier; anyway the news is new to me. Then the word *old* seemed to stay in my mind, and I wondered what my *Merriam-Webster Dictionary* would say about that word, so I looked it up. Now, I found several definitions, which gave me food for thought. OLDadj. 1:ANCIENT, also:of long standing. 2: belonging to an early period. 3: having existed for a specified period of time. 4: advanced in years. There were a few more, but I figured I knew the true meaning, so I closed my dictionary and began thinking about that word, *old*.

I'm eighty-six, and according to the Bible, in Luke 2:36–37 (NIV), when Jesus was being dedicated eight days after His birth, there was a woman prophetess named Anna, who had lived at the temple for years, and it states "that she was very old and her age was 84." So I guess that indicates that I'm old. Actually that doesn't upset me, as I'm in fairly good health, can still walk, do my own cooking, and take care of the house and my husband. So I won't complain about being old. That makes me think of the old year, 2016, and the New Year of 2017.

There is a verse in the Bible, 2 Corinthians 5:17 that says, "Therefore, if anyone is in Christ, he is a new creation; the old has gone, the new has come."(NIV) Like the year 2016, it has gone, and 2017 is here and it is brand-new. I know that that verse is referring to a person, meaning that if we accept Christ and make Him part of our lives, we are like a different person; the old way of living is gone and the new *you* is here. I was thinking that if we want to have a great New Year in 2017, perhaps if we put off the old things we did in 2016 and let Christ be a part of the coming year, things could be different. I think I'll try to make a few resolutions for 2017 by putting off some of the old things I did in 2016 and try putting God first in my life. I'm not going to look to the past but to the future. Won't you join with me in turning over a new leaf like that verse says—"the old is gone the new is here"? And that's my New Year's resolution for 2017, direct from my kitchen table.

Letter #12

Whether or Not to Enjoy January Weather

January 6, 2017

I'M ONCE AGAIN SITTING AT MY KITCHEN TABLE looking at the blanket of snow on the lawn out back. We were supposed to get more snow last night, but we only got a blanket to cover the ground. Roads are good here, but down in the southern tier, they have a foot or more of snow, and on TV it looks like they are snowed in. Schools are closed, and cars are buried in some places, with traffic at a standstill. At this time of the year we can expect snow, so it's not unusual to hear those bad weather reports. As for me, I don't plan on venturing out.

The old year went without much fanfare, and the New Year arrived in the same way, sort of slid in with wonderfully mild temperatures to make the start of this year a pleasant one. I'm hoping that this January will be calm and peaceful. I've had several Januarys that were very, very bad—such as the blizzard of 1977 and the bad snowstorm in 1986 when my husband, Richard, was superintendent of highways. I didn't see him for days, but I saw plenty of extra people who kept me busy. Both times we had people stranded here, which made for exciting times. During the blizzard of '77, our septic line from the house to the tank was frozen, as it was so cold out, but I was able to catch the flushes in a pail in the basement, which I had to empty every hour, and that was no pleasant task. I had to dress in snow clothes, headgear, and boots to keep from freezing, as the wind was so strong and the snow knee-deep. Fortunately, I had plenty of food to feed those three extra adults and three children for the entire week they were here. Sleeping arrangements were also good, as we had plenty of floor space, beds, and blankets.

Once again in '86 we had people snowed in; there were six extra adults—two women and four men—who had been drinking all afternoon, and this was 6:30 at night. The snow and wind were so bad you couldn't see the road or the neighbor across the road. I couldn't send them away in such weather, so I fed them, talked to them, we played cards and put a puzzle together, and finally I bedded them down at 12:00 midnight. It made for a very interesting night. You know in the Bible, in Hebrews 13: 2, it says, "Do not forget to entertain strangers, for by so doing some people have entertained angels without knowing it."(NIV) I don't know if they were angels, but that was one January snowstorm I won't forget.

Being the wife of a superintendent of highways was always different in the winter, and those last two weeks in January seemed to have the worst weather. Except for March 17, St. Patrick's Day, it would always storm. It was one of the last—and usually the worst—storm of the year. Now that Richard is retired, we don't worry about the weather. In the Bible, in Matthew 6:34, it says, "Therefore do not worry about tomorrow, for tomorrow will worry about itself. Each day has enough trouble of its own."(NIV) Good advice for this year of 2017—not to worry but to trust God for His provisions and care. Being retired does have its advantages: no more roads to plow or snow to be concerned about. When it storms, we simply stay put. I can enjoy the January weather and snow, resting in God's love and care at my favorite spot, of course, right here at my kitchen table.

Letter #13

The Many Things That Make Us Think of Love

February 1, 2017

ONCE AGAIN I'M SITTING AT MY KITCHEN TABLE after returning from Batavia. We had to go pick up our prescriptions at CVS and then some quick shopping at Walmart. When we finished shopping, we grabbed a quick bite to eat at Subway, which turned out to be a real blessing. We ordered subs, coffee, and chips, and while enjoying our meal, we decided that the soft pretzel, served hot with cheese dip, looked good too. I fell in line behind this young girl as she ordered her sub, and she also ordered a pretzel. When I ordered my pretzel, the girl behind the counter put both of the pretzels in the oven at the same time to warm. The young girl proceeded to pay for her meal as we waited for our pretzels to warm, and then she turned to the cashier and told her she would pay for my pretzel as well. I said, "No, that isn't necessary," but she insisted, so I smiled and thanked her for her kindness. It really made me feel good to know that there are still young people in this world who have love and kindness in their hearts. It made my day.

This also brought to mind that special day of love, Valentine's Day—which was coming—and brought back many memories of when I was younger. I then began to think about the word *love* and what some signs of love are. When we see a heart, we think of love, or cupid on a card makes one think of love. How about a picture of lips forming a kiss? Once again we think of love. Watching a young couple walking hand in hand or witnessing a bride and groom saying their vows, again that word *love* pops up in our minds. I also pictured a cross, and that made me think of love. So much love Jesus had for me and you that He willing submitted to going to the cross and giving His life for my sins that I might have life everlasting. That truly was love, and it was unconditional.

Then I went to my trusty dictionary to find out the meaning of that word, *love*, and there were several; but I'll only name a few. Love n. "1: CHERISH 2: to feel a passion, devotion, or tenderness for 3: attraction based on sexual desire 4: a beloved person 5: a score of zero in tennis." That last one was a real letdown for me. Noticing my Bible on the table, I decided to look there, and this is what I came up with, which I think is a very good answer. In the New Testament, turn to 1 Corinthians 13:4–8a, which describes the word *love*: "Love is patient, love is kind, does not envy, or boast. It is not proud, or rude, or self-seeking. Does not get angry, keeps no record of wrong, does not delight in evil, but rejoices in truth. Love always protects, trusts, hopes and perseveres. Love never fails." (NIV) Wow! Now that is a good description of love; at least I think it is. Hopefully, I can have that kind of love in my heart now and always. Hope you too will have that kind of love in your heart, not only on Valentine's Day but all year long. Now pour yourself another cup of coffee and join me at my kitchen table.

Letter #14

A Fun-Filled Trip and Back Home Again

March 1, 2017

I'M HOME, AND DOES IT EVER FEEL GOOD JUST TO sit at my beautiful kitchen table and enjoy time alone. Actually it was a wonderful trip. My son Ken lives in North Carolina, but he travels all the time preaching to the youth at camps and churches all over America and in Europe. So when he is home, we take advantage of the fact and go to visit him and his family. All his children are married and have children, with three of his four children living in North Carolina in the same area. His fourth child lives in Germany and is a missionary there. My son Tracy's daughter, Julie, is married and lives in Virginia, so we had planned on stopping there first before proceeding to North Carolina. We didn't plan on driving all that distance by ourselves, because of our age, so our oldest daughter, Mona, was going along to help with the driving. Since we have a Chevy Uplander that seats seven, my grand-daughter Teri and her two girls, Miranda and Macy, who had vacation from

Oakfield School that week, were invited to go along. Then at the last minute my daughter Betty was able to get off work, and she joined us on our trip. With the van packed with five adults, two children, suitcases, sleeping bags, and pillows, we left early on Friday morning.

Virginia was our first stop to see Julie and Andrew and their new baby girl, whom we had never seen nor held. She's our little miracle great-grand daughter born two months early, weighting two pounds, six ounces, and we were anxious to see her for the first time. Nine hours and four hundred miles later, we arrived in Virginia, tired but excited to be there. What a great time we had with Julie, Andrew, and Emily, who is now a healthy seven-pound bright-eyed little girl and two months old. Oh, how we hated to leave, but we only had a week, so we needed to travel on to our next stop: Durham, North Carolina.

We headed for Durham, North Carolina, with Teri driving. Many hours later we arrived at Chris's home and his family of six was in the front yard to greet us. What a happy welcome as we once again greeted loved ones. Chris has three daughters and one son, and with our two little girls, they all had a fun-filled time of playing together as we adults talked and shared past times together. The time went swiftly for us, and three days later, we said our happy, tearful goodbyes.

But first we stopped off for lunch with some dear friends, the Rodlands, as they were right on our way to my son's place. Dorie served us our first picnic of 2017, and much to our delight, it was Salen hot dogs done on the grill. Needless to say, it was great seeing those dear folks once more.

As Charlotte, North Carolina, came into view, Mona called attention to the great dam built there, which looked like a great wall. She told the two little girls, "Look at that wall holding back all that water." Six-year-old Macy looked and commented,

"Well, I guess Trump did build his wall!" which proves that kids are listening all the time, so watch what you say.

Our three days with our son and daughter-in-law, Ken and Jinner, were filled with visits from our grand-son Ben and his family, who live next door, and grand-daughter Trisha and her family, who live a short distance up the street. It was great to see everyone again, and we filled each moment with games, conversation, laughter, eating, and remembering. Then once again our tearful goodbyes and a prayer for safe travel, and then we were on our way home. It was a long twelve-hour drive, which was shared by Mona and Teri, and the closer we got to home, the excitement grew. I think that's the way it will be when the Lord calls us home to our home in heaven. John 14:2 says, "In my Father's house are many rooms; if it were not so I would have told you. I'm going to prepare a place for you." (NIV) What a joy to know that Jesus is preparing a place for me—a home in heaven, where I'll no longer be sitting at my kitchen table but at the banquet table with Him, enjoying those heavenly comforts.

Letter #15

Three Days Without Electricity

March 15, 2017

WELL, I REALLY DID SIT AT MY KITCHEN TABLE FOR three days without the blessings of electricity. Yes, that windstorm that roared through here on Wednesday, March 8, hit with a vengeance. I don't mind a snowstorm without wind, as that can be peaceful and pretty, but when God adds wind to it, there is trouble.

We were safe and sound until 4:24 p.m. on Wednesday when our electric went out, and we weren't too concerned until about an hour later when we reported our outage to the power company. They were aware of our situation but said they didn't know when the electricity would be returning. My husband, Richard, decided to get our generator hooked up so we would have heat and lights. He called our daughter Mona next door, and she came over to help get the generator hooked up at our house and stay with us to keep warm, as she didn't have electricity either. It took them about thirty minutes to get everything hooked up and going.

The next three days passed ever so slowly as we hunkered down to enjoy the time to be together in just the kitchen and dining area of our home, as the generator wasn't large enough to provide heat and power to the entire house. Of course at nighttime we stopped the generator, as it didn't hold enough gas to run through the night. We layered ourselves with extra sweaters, jeans, socks, and blankets, crawled under the covers, and slept really well. The temperature in the kitchen/dining room/bedroom areas never got below 59 degrees. We decided to go out for meals, as the electric range took too much juice, and if that ran at the same time as our water pump, it would blow out the 220, and then we couldn't flush the toilets. We could do only one thing at a time, but we did manage to stay warm, played games, watched TV, and got to go out for meals.

Why is it we take our electricity for granted? Do we feel entitled to electricity because we pay for it? When it's out, we finally realize how much we miss that wonderful thing called *electricity*. We get impatient with the electric company because we are inconvenienced for awhile. National Grid had people working day and night to get it going, and do we say thank you to them for all their hard work, or do we complain that we had a little discomfort for a few days? Yes, I did sit at my kitchen table without electricity, but fortunately we did have that little generator, and we were very thankful when the electricity was returned. We sent a prayer of thanks to God and a big thank-you to National Grid for its return.

It's like the way we treat God. We take Him for granted, and we don't have to pay for God's care. Often, we forget to pray and talk with Him or read His Word. We have many excuses, we don't have time, or we put it off until tomorrow. Yes, God patiently waits for us to come to Him and give Him a few minutes of our time. Yet when trouble happens or we get sick, then we find time to pray.

From now on I intend on being thankful to National Grid, the telephone company, and others who are of service to me, but most of all to my precious Lord for His love and salvation. In Hebrews 12:28b, it says, "Let us be thankful and so worship God acceptably with reverence and awe."(NIV) Guess I'll do just that, right here at my kitchen table.

Letter #16

Love of God and Love of Family

March 23, 2017

I'M SITTING AT MY KITCHEN TABLE TONIGHT WITH some twenty other members of our family joining with me to celebrate the March birthdays. It's my husband Richard's ninety-second birthday; our daughter Betty's birthday; the birthdays of three grand-sons—Brett, Randy, and Andrew—and the birthdays of two great-grand children: Lincoln (in Germany) and Hallie (in North Carolina). The laughter and conversation fill the room as babies, kids, and people of all ages join us at this special Sunday night meal, with birthday cake and pie later. My heart is overflowing with gratitude to God for giving us time together as a family to celebrate all those with March birthdays. I'm thankful for God's love and the many blessings He has given me during these many years of my life, and once more I'm happy to be sitting at my kitchen table while I let the rest wait on me. The chatter and laughter are sometimes loud, and the crying of a baby adds to the celebration as we finish the meal, sing all the happy birthdays, blow out the candles, enjoy the cakes and pies, and open the gifts. God is good, and we are having a wonderful time. A time filled with the love of God and love of family—yes, love; that is what makes the world go round.

I'm so thankful that God arranged for us to be in families. Many centuries ago God placed Adam and Eve in the Garden of Eden as husband and wife, and they started a family with Cain and Abel. Families were from the beginning, and I'm thankful for that. I was born into a large, loving family, and I am thankful that God saw fit for me to be married to a man who also came from a loving family. That love of God and love of family have been passed down through the years, and I hope and pray that my children, grand-children, and great-grand-children will continue to pass down that love in the years to come. In John 3:16 it says, "For God so loved the world that he gave his one and only Son, that whoever believes in him, shall not perish but have eternal life."(NIV) Yes, two thousand years ago this wonderful God passed down to us His Son, Jesus, who was willing to die for us that we might have life forever. And many centuries ago, God arranged for us to live as families and share His love with each other.

So as I watch this celebration from my kitchen table, I'm hoping that all of you who are reading this will be as blessed as I am and able to celebrate the love of God and the love of family at your next birthday party or any other event.

Jean and Richard with their four children and spouses

Letter #17

Thankful That Spring Has Come

April 17, 2017

WELL, IT MUST OFFICIALLY BE SPRING, AS MY HUSband mowed the lawn today for the very first time in 2017. As I sat at my kitchen table, I could observe him on that trusty John Deere tractor as he went back and forth from east to west in perfect rows. He actually looked like he was enjoying himself. Even though the thermometer was at 59, that wonderful wind, which seems to be part of western New York, made it cold enough to bundle up and enjoy the warmth of his winter jacket. What a sight to see him mowing a lawn all bundled up like it was winter.

Actually Richard had been out for the last two days picking up twigs, branches, debris, and leaves just to get ready to mow; that was the hard part. The mowing is the easy job. Since retiring, he welcomes summer months when he has work to do. Actually he mows the church lawns too, which consist of six acres, including "Samuel's Field" next to the parsonage, which is where they have baseball games and where kids run and play in the summer.

I think God gave us spring to make us appreciate His beautiful world. The different seasons make us thankful for each one, happy to see one season go and another come. Spring is here, and as the trees bud and bloom, they seem to say "Hello" as they turn from buds to leaves. The differently colored greens say, "Welcome! How about taking a walk?" Actually those crabapple trees with their white and pink blossoms and those yellow forsythia bushes, along with daffodils and hyacinths, fairly shout, "Spring is here!" So get out of the house and enjoy that new life that spring brings. Ecclesiastes 3:1 says, "There's a time for everything, and a season for every activity under heaven."(NIV) Yes, spring is one of those seasons! Guess I'll leave my kitchen table, grab my spring jacket, and take a walk in God's beautiful outdoors. Won't you join me there?

Letter #18

Honor Your Father and Mother

May 10, 2017

ACTUALLY I'M SITTING AT MY KITCHEN TABLE reading the ads from the newspaper, and most of them are shouting that it is Mother's Day this coming Sunday. All the ads and commercials on the TV are suggesting that you better get shopping soon, as you need to buy something for your mother. All those reminders sort of make me sad, as my mom is no longer with me and I'm sitting here reminiscing about those days when I was a little girl. I'm now a mom, grandma, and great-grandma, but some of those memories of my mother are still fresh in my mind.

My mom, Clara Klotzbach, always wore an apron with pockets, where she had a clean white hanky for us little ones to blow our nose; no Kleenex around at that time. She often hummed hymns while she worked around the kitchen. She was soft and smelled like Sweetheart soap when you snuggled close, and it didn't matter that you were too big for her lap; you were always welcomed with a hug and a kiss. She wore her hair combed back in a bun, and it was always neat and clean. She didn't wear makeup, as her cheeks were rosy and her complexion flawless; her eyes were gray-blue with that special twinkle. She never shouted when disciplining us but was strict and firm and relied on a small cherry switch when it was needed. I don't ever remember hearing my mom and dad argue or raise their voices to each other. She was a wonderful cook and baker, and she did a lot of that. She loved to crochet and was a great seamstress. She was my friend as well as my mother, and I'll always be grateful that I had such a wonderful mom. I was the tenth child in a family of thirteen children, but I never felt neglected or unloved. She was the best mom in the world, and I lost her when she was only sixty-five years old and I was twenty-eight.

So my message to you is to love your mom, appreciate her, visit her often, and enjoy every minute you have together. Giving her a material gift is a good idea, but sometimes just the giving of your time is more of a blessing to her, especially as one gets older. In the Bible, in Exodus 20:12, it says, "Honor your father and your mother, so that you may live long in the land the Lord your God is giving you."(NIV) This is the Fifth Commandment that God gave us; it's not just me reminding you to love your mother, it's God telling you to do so. If for some reason there is trouble or things aren't good between you and your mom, why not forget past mistakes and start over? Don't wait until it's too late and she is gone. Forgive and let by-gones be by- gones. Remember, this is what God would have you do. And that's remembering my mom from my kitchen table.

Letter #19

Remembering Those Who Gave Their Lives

May 22, 2017

TODAY AS WE FINISHED OUR MORNING DEVOTIONS at the kitchen table, I realized that one week from today we will be celebrating Memorial Day, or Decoration Day, as it was called when I was little. On that holiday, Mom would cut lilacs off the lilac bush and take the flowers to the cemeteries and decorate all the graves of her relatives in the North Pembroke cemetery. Then she would cut more lilacs for my father's relatives in the Indian Falls cemetery and Corfu cemetery. This was also the beginning of summer and the planting of crops for us farmers.

The decorating of graves of fallen soldiers of the Civil War began in 1864 and was the start of this celebration, originally called Decoration Day. The name changed down through the years to Memorial Day, as did the date. May 30 was the original date, but in 1968 Congress changed the date from the traditional day to the last Monday in the month of May, which would create a three-day weekend, and that became a law in 1971. I found all this information and much more when I went on the Internet. Yes, Memorial Day is a tribute to all soldiers and others who have served in some way and a day to remember family and friends who are no longer with us. We realize that freedom is not free, as it cost the lives of many dear ones who gave their lives that we might be free from tyranny and injustice. What a gift! And many don't pause to remember the cost or say thank you.

Another one who has given me so much at a great cost of His life is mentioned in the Bible, in Galatians 2:20d, where Paul writes, "I have faith in the Son of God, who loved me and gave himself for me."(NIV) Yes, Jesus died on that cross many years ago that I might have a home in heaven someday, and He did it not only for me but for all who believe. On this Memorial Day, why not take a few moments to thank Jesus, who died for you and me, and also those brave soldiers who gave their lives that we might have these freedoms we have today? And that's the way it looks from my kitchen table.

Letter #20

Blessed to Have Completed My Bible Course

May 27, 2017

LAST WEEK I FINALLY FINISHED THE BIBLE COURSE I've been taking for several years, and I'm now a "Certified Lay Servant," which means I'm qualified by the United Methodist Church to speak in other churches. I first started this study when Rev. Ken Dodd was our pastor, which was a position he held for sixteen years. I think he would have been happy to continue as our pastor, but the Lord saw fit to relieve Ken from His earthly duties and take him to his heavenly home. Pastor Ken had asked me to take this course, and I started it but could never find the time to complete it. There was either no teacher or not enough people interested in taking the course, or I was on vacation when it was offered, and even the weather interfered with snow cancellations.

Then this past April, our present pastor, Karen Grinnell, offered to teach a class for the completion of this study. I felt like she did it especially for me, but when class began, there were thirteen signed up. Needless to say we all had a great ten hours of study and renewing of our faith as we looked into God's Word together. I'm very thankful that I could finish this course and complete it in honor of Ken Dodd, who had great faith in me to be able to speak in other churches and bring the message of God's love, hope, and faith to others. In Mark 16:15 Jesus said, "Go, into all the world and preach the good news to all creation."(NIV) And now I'm certified to do so.

Writing these letters to the editor has been a great way for me to share some of my thoughts and happenings in my life with others, and the *Daily News* has been more than gracious in printing my letters. Many people have told me how much they enjoy my kitchen table letters, and that has been a joy for me to hear. Please don't think I'm bragging; I'm just thankful that we have a paper that will let us say what we think and publish it. I know I'm not always English-perfect but I do so enjoy sharing my faith and thoughts with others in this way. I'm a people person and enjoy fellowshipping with others, and what better way than around the table with the home town newspaper.

Letter #21

Computers Make It Possible to Keep in Touch

June 1, 2017

JUST RETURNED HOME FROM HAVING BREAKFAST with some dear friends, Tony and Peg. It was so good seeing them once again and renewing old friendships. We hadn't seen them in a really long time, so it was extra-special as we shared about families and friends. When one is retired, one tends to get caught up in the everyday happenings of life and sometimes we forget to stop and smell the roses.

This makes me grateful that I have the Internet and Facebook. I can keep up with family and friends whether they are near or far from home. When I retired for the second time, from working at the Akron Bank, I decided to invest in a computer, as I loved the one at work and knew a little bit about using one. Lucky for me I found a great computer guy, Drew, who helped me purchase the best computer and taught me how to use it and set it up. For these past eleven years, I've really enjoyed my computer and have used it almost every day. Even though I've sometimes shouted at it and called it names, I love keeping in touch with friends and relatives all over America and even in countries across the ocean. I may be old, but I don't have to sit back and let life pass me by.

God gave me life and has seen fit to let me live for many, many years. Even though it's hard for me to stand or walk, I'm thankful to be able to do my housework, get meals, go places, eat out, and enjoy being alive. So, just a little advice to all you elderly ones like me. Don't just sit and rock your life away; read, keep your mind sharp, call a friend on the phone, visit with others, go to church, write letters to the editor, go to the mall and walk, and don't forget to pray. That keeps you in touch with the *One* who cares the most for you and loves you no matter who you are; young, middle-aged, or old, you can depend on Him. In 1 Thessalonians 5:16–18 it says, "Be joyful always; Pray continually; Give thanks in all circumstances, for this is God's will for you in Christ Jesus."(NIV) Yes, and please keep sitting with me at my kitchen table, as I do so enjoy visiting with all of you.

Letter #22

Some Weather Thoughts

June 12, 2017

I'M SITTING AT MY KITCHEN TABLE AND REALIZED that today, June 12, would be my brother Roy Klotzbach's birthday if he were alive. Today is really warm—it's almost 80 degrees out—and that got me to reminiscing about something that my mother told me many years ago. When Roy was born on June 12, 1918, that day dawned cold and windy with two inches of snow covering the ground, and my dad was planting potatoes that day, with a winter overcoat and gloves on, as it was so cold. Now today it's warm and sunny; what a difference almost one hundred years makes.

Just proves that here in western New York one never knows what the weather will be. My husband, Richard, always says, "If you don't like the weather here in western New York, just wait ten minutes and it will change." Even with all that said, I don't want to live anywhere else. We have wind but not tornadoes. Snow, but that will melt sooner or later. Complaining about the weather won't change it, as God is in charge of the weather, so we might as well enjoy what comes our way.

Our Methodist Church, in Indian Falls, was given the gift of air-conditioning by an anonymous donor, so this summer our church services should be very comfortable and cool. No excuses for not attending church because it's hot. It won't be too hot, and it won't be too cold either. Those in our congregation who are going to be running it have pledged to make it a comfortable temperature, hopefully to please one and all. Actually I was happy to have the windows open and the breezes blowing in, even if it was a little uncomfortable a couple of times in the summer. Psalm 122:1 says, "I rejoiced with those who said to me, 'Let us go to the house of the Lord.'"(NIV) So that's what I'll do: rejoice that I can go to church without fear and have the right to worship as I choose. That's some weather thoughts from my kitchen table, whether you like them or not.

Letter #23

Singing Throughout the Summer Months

August 3, 2017

IT'S ALREADY AUGUST. WHERE DID THE TIME GO? Can't believe that summer is half over and fall will soon be here. It's been a busy summer but actually not one where we have gone on vacation or something earth shaking—just everyday life. But thank God it has not been a boring one. We have managed to go places, visit our children, enjoy meals with friends and loved ones, go to church events, go to doctor's appointments, and babysit some of our great-grandchildren. When one is busy, it keeps one from being depressed. Richard still mows the lawns at church, and I keep busy with housework, cooking, and writing on my computer. Life is *good*, even if I do have a few aches and pains.

This past Sunday my cousin Barb Kern, my daughter Betty Hall, and I were privileged to sing in our church as a trio. Actually we've been singing together for about the last twenty years, and every summer we are asked to do special music for one of the Sundays in the summer months, since our choir takes a vacation. So all summer on Sundays we have someone different bring the message in song during the service. We sang three numbers, one for the Prelude, one for the Anthem, and one for the Offertory. Since we sang, I've been singing those songs over and over again these past few days. The first one we sang was titled "Change My Heart O God," and it keeps running through my mind, and I find myself singing it over and over again. It's almost like a prayer, and it goes like this: "Change my heart O God, make it ever new, change my heart O God, may I be like You." This morning as I was sitting at my kitchen table, once again I was singing and praying those words. I really would like to be more like Him: kind, loving, forgiving, patient, and always ready to listen. I know that God is the potter and I'm the clay, and He will mold me into the person He wants me to be if I willingly turn my life over to Him. In Ephesians 5:19b it tells us to "Sing and make music in your heart to the Lord."(NIV) Yes, God wants me to sing and make music as a way to praise Him. Guess I'll do that, as it's a joy for me to be able to sing at church and praise the Lord—or even right here at my kitchen table.

Letter #24

Anniversary—A Chance to Reminisce

August 25, 2017

I'M SITTING AT MY KITCHEN TABLE AND REMEM-bering last Sunday and the good time we had celebrating with our old friends Hank and Norma Kelver, who were observing their seventieth wedding anniversary. My husband, Richard, and the Kelvers go back many years, at least seventy-five, but I've only known them for about sixty-nine years. Anyway, we had a great time, as their children (five sons) and their wives surprised them with a great party held at the Harris Corners Fire Hall. About a hundred people, family and friends, gathered for a wonderful meal and to catch up on past years. Many memories and some old pictures from their wedding were enjoyed by all who attended.

Richard was their best man at that August 23 wedding, and he remembers that it was a really warm night with temperatures at about 90 degrees, in the Alexander Methodist Church. Reminiscing about such a beautiful occasion brought back memories of how they pledged their love that day and also honored that love for seventy years. Needless to say, it was a joyous celebration. We've stayed in touch with them for these many years and are so thankful for friends such as they. There is an old saying that goes like this: "Make new friends but keep the old, one is silver and the other gold." I like that saying, and I definitely agree with it.

One friend who I keep in touch with everyday is probably the best friend anyone could have. Yes, I'm talking about my friend Jesus, and what He did for me more than two thousand years ago. In John 15:13 it says, "Greater love has no one than this, that he lay down his life for his friends."(NIV) And that's exactly what Jesus did for all of us, so I try to keep in touch with Him every day through prayer and reading His Word, thanking Him for His love and care and all the many blessings I receive from Him every day. It's a joy to talk with Him and know that He is there for me anytime of the day or night. Guess you could say he is that "gold friend" and priceless. Well, I better say goodbye and put my reminiscing away for now. Thanks again for joining me at my kitchen table for a short visit and that second cup of coffee.

Letter #25

Offering to Take a Stand for the Lord

September 6, 2017

SEVERAL WEEKS AGO I TOLD YOU HOW I FINISHED that course in becoming a Lay Servant Ministry Speaker, and now I want to tell you that I received the chance to use that certification. On August 27, I was privileged to bring the message at my church here in Indian Falls. It was a joy to tell others about our job as Christians and disciples of Jesus, that we should be going into the world and proclaiming the Good News to all nations. Jesus gave this command in Matthew 28:19–20: "Therefore go and make disciples of all nations, baptizing them in the name of the Father and of the Son and of the Holy Spirit, and teaching them to obey everything I have commanded you. And surely I am with you always, to the very end if the age."(NIV) It was not a suggestion but a command to all who love the Lord and want to do His will.

Now my world is right here in western New York, and I feel I have been doing this from my kitchen table through my letters. It's been a fun time for me, and from all the notes and responses from people wherever I go, I guess some of you have enjoyed my letters as well. Thank you for reading my letters. I feel like you have become my friends and part of my family through these letters. I feel honored to have them published and grateful that I can share my love for Jesus with all of you in this special way. I want to be a servant and disciple who is willing to take a stand for my Lord and tell others about His unfailing love and grace. What a joy to spread the Word right here in my world of western New York.

Let me say that you are welcome at my kitchen table anytime you read my letters, as I do so enjoy sharing the Good News with you. Thank you, *Daily News*, for allowing me to use this special place on page four of your newspaper. Now, pour yourself that second cup of coffee, grab a cookie or two, and join me at my kitchen table.

Letter #26

Recent Hurricanes Are a
Signal from God

September 10, 2017

CAN'T BELIEVE THAT ANOTHER HURRICANE IS headed toward the Keys of Florida, and some of the people are already headed out for places of safety. I can't imagine what they are going through and how very scared they must be. Hurricane Harvey was a mega one and the destruction is awful, and many families have lost their homes and everything they owned. What does one do when all that is left of your home is a pile of junk? Many brave souls have reported that they are going to be all right; their homes and possessions are gone, but their family members are still alive, and no one was hurt, so they will just rebuild. How? They don't know, but they will survive in this crazy world.

Hurricane Irma hit Florida with a vengeance, and the destruction is worse than anticipated. Some places, such as the Keys, are underwater, and bridges, roads, and homes are no longer in view. Other parts of Florida are untouched and going on as usual. Many people have gone down there to help, and I thank all the volunteers who are able to give of their services. America truly is a great nation of people ready and willing to lend a hand when needed. The loss of life is few and we thank God for His protection during this time of disaster.

Why do hurricanes, earthquakes, fires, and tornados happen? I don't know, but they do, and we need to look up when all these natural disasters happen and get right with God. He's trying to get our attention that we as a nation must get back to worshipping Him as we did centuries ago. Our nation was founded on the principle of "one nation under God," but somewhere along the line we have forgotten this motto. In the Bible, in 2 Chronicles 7:14, it says, "If my people, who are called by my name, will humble themselves and pray and seek my face and turn from their wicked ways, then I will hear from heaven, and I will forgive their sins and heal their land."(NIV) Sounds like it might work if we get back to praising God and worshipping Him as a nation. I would really like for America to give it a try. I think I'll start by being more dedicated to praying for America and asking God for His blessings on all of us, as we strive to live for Him, and if you would join me each day right here at my kitchen table in doing the same, it might work.

Letter #27

Take Time to Enjoy and Celebrate God's Autumn

October 1, 2017

OCTOBER IS HERE, AND FOR ME THAT IS ONE SPE-cial month. I have two great-granddaughters, Eliza and Olivia, who have birthdays, as does my son Tracy. Also my birthday and our anniversary are in October. I have two sisters-in-law, nieces, friends, and a cousin who share birthdays in October, and my "special" great-niece, Corinne Phelps, also celebrates a birthday. What a joy to celebrate birthdays, as well as my sixty-ninth anniversary. I really don't mind getting old, as that means I'm still alive and God doesn't need me as yet, for which I am grateful.

I was married at eighteen, and I know there were several people who thought I was much too young and that it couldn't possibly last. Fortunately, I married a wonderful man who loved me very much, and he promised before God to "take me for better or for worse." I too made that same promise, and we have honored those words ever since. Of course we have had our disagreements at times, which is to be expected in any marriage, but love wins out in the end. There have been times when Richard has said, "I wouldn't take a million dollars for Jean, and yet there are some days I would give her away." Might I say that there have been times when I have felt the same way about Richard. Marriage is a give-and-take situation, and some days you give more than you get, but with a kiss and a plea for forgiveness, those times can vanish.

Now for all of you out there who read my letters, may October be a special month for all of you. It's a beautiful month, with the leaves changing color and the crisp, cool air of fall. It's a beautiful prelude to the winter months ahead. It's harvest time, and the bounty that the Lord has provided for us gives us cause to offer thanks for living in this beautiful country. May you enjoy this time of red, yellow, and brown leaves, of golden sunrises and sunsets, and of red apples and golden pears, and praise God for His love and glorious gifts of autumn. It's almost as if the earth were singing and making melody for all of us to enjoy. In Isaiah 14: 7 it says, "The whole earth is at rest, and is quiet: they break forth into singing."(KJV) Guess that's a good idea, breaking forth into singing praises to God, and I can do that right here at my kitchen table.

Letter #28

A Special Trip with My Adult Family

October 17, 2017

WELL, I'M NOT SITTING AT MY KITCHEN TABLE, AS we're on our way home from a fast overnight trip to Clarks Summit, Pennsylvania. It was a spur-of-the-moment trip when we found out that our son Kenneth would be speaking on Friday at Clarks Summit University, over homecoming weekend. Ken went to college there and graduated in 1975. Ken and his wife, Jinner, now live in North Carolina, and we don't see him very often or get a chance to hear him preach. Clarks Summit is only a five-hour trip, so we decided to travel that short distance to see them and also to be able to hear him preach in chapel. Of course our children won't let us travel alone, as we're elderly, and our eldest daughter, Mona, was happy to volunteer to drive us down. Then our daughter Betty decided it was a good idea to ride along, and when our son Tracy heard about our plans, he too wanted in on our family trip.

Now, this was the first time in many years that this mom and dad got to travel with three of their adult children; only this time instead of us taking care of them, they were taking care of us. It was a joyous trip, and we laughed and reminisced all the way. We arrived at 3:15 p.m., and Ken was there to welcome us. We got settled in our rooms, visited for awhile, and then went to pick up Ken's wife, Jinner, who was visiting at a friend's home.

We had a fun evening, as Richard and I took our four adult children and daughter-in-law out for dinner, and then we had a joyful time of fellowship back at the motel. This got me to thinking how happy it must make God when His children get together and worship Him with singing and praise and prayer. My heart was bursting with love having all four children together, so I can imagine that God is overjoyed when His family members come to Him in prayer and visit with Him.

Yes, we had a glorious time these past two days, but as wonderful as it is to travel and see loved ones, it's even better to go home. And that's the way it'll be when we leave this earth and go home to heaven. Our travel time here on earth is short compared to what eternity will be; a home where we will live forever. In 2 Corinthians 5:1 it says, "Now we know that if this earthly tent we live in is destroyed, we have a building from God, an eternal home in heaven, not built by human hands."(NIV) Jesus paid the price for that heavenly home by laying down His life on the cross and paying for our salvation. Our part is to accept Him as our Savior so that we may have life everlasting. As I write from my kitchen table, I'll keep praying and reading God's Word, and when my time comes to "Really Go Home," I'll be ready.

Letter #29

Choosing to Be a "Thanks-Giver"

November 17, 2017

Today the air is nippy and crisp, but there's no snow. It's already halfway through November, and we've only had a sprinkling of snow, at least outside my kitchen window. I'm thankful that so far this year we've had beautiful fall weather. Of course, I've heard that this is going to be a bad winter for snow, and yet others have predicted that "when we have rain and thunder in the fall, it means no winter at all." Guess we'll have to wait and see what God has in store for us. I know when I was younger I really liked the snow and cold. Going to work or to church and driving in the snow never bothered me; I was game for anything. Now I'm more timid about venturing out.

In just a few short days we'll be celebrating Thanksgiving, which is always a fun time with food and fellowship and also a time to pause and thank God for His bountiful goodness to us. In 1 Chronicles 16:34 it says, "Give thanks to the Lord, for he is good; his love endures forever."(NIV) Yes, I'm thankful that God has provided for us and blessed us so much with His grace and love. So many times we get busy and forget to pray and read our Bible, but God never forgets us; He's always there waiting to hear from us. So this Thanksgiving won't you take a few moments to pause before you gobble all that turkey and trimmings and be a thanks-giver. And I'll be joining with you to do the same right here at my kitchen table.

Letter #30
The Meaning of Christmas

December 1, 2017

THE OTHER DAY, AT MY KITCHEN TABLE, I GOT TO thinking that if I had to describe Christmas by using only one word, what would that word be? Actually I don't think there is one word that could describe such a wonderful time of the year, but I wrote down several that I thought might come close, such as *exciting, wonderful, magnificent, gifts, awesome, holy, joyous,* and *beautiful,* but none of them actually described Christmas. Then that little four-letter word *love* popped into mind, and I knew that that was the word closest to describing Christmas: *love.*

Actually love was the true meaning of the very first Christmas. That tiny baby boy named Jesus, wrapped in cloths and laid in a manger, was God's gift of love to the whole world. And God knew that that precious gift of His Son, Jesus, would be the only way to bring His love to the sin-sick people of the world. Luke 2:7 says, "And she brought forth her first born son, and wrapped him in swaddling clothes, and laid him in a manger; because there was no room for them in the inn."(KJV)

Yes, love in the form of a tiny baby boy came down at Christmas more than two thousand years ago, and today we are still celebrating that love each and every Christmas, as well as all year long. That gift of love was wrapped in strips of cloth, as there were no blankets, and then laid in a manger full of hay, as there was no crib. Yet, there was something special as shepherds came to worship Him and wise men came to bring Him gifts.

What a wonderful time of year as we celebrate our Savior's birth by singing carols and giving gifts. My prayer for all of you is that His love will fill your hearts and you'll let the true meaning of Christmas fill your soul with love for Him and then give that gift of love to others. Now, from my kitchen table, let me wish you all a Merry Christmas.

Letter #31
A Valuable Gift to Open at Christmas

December 11, 2017

I WASN'T GOING TO SEND ANOTHER LETTER PER-taining to Christmas, but when I read this story about a gift, I had to share it with all of you.

It's a story about a rich father and his teenage son. The son was about to graduate from high school and was hoping for a beautiful red car he'd seen in the show room of the car dealer in town. He kept telling his dad what a great car it was and how much he wanted it for his graduation gift. The day he graduated, his father, handed the son a small wrapped package to open. The son was very disappointed but opened it only to discover that it was a Bible. He angrily threw the Bible on his father's desk and shouted, with harsh words, "I don't need this book! All I wanted was a car! You could afford a car; you are such a tightwad!" And with that the son left the house and never returned.

Many years passed, and the son had made a good life for himself. One day he received news that his father had passed away and that he was left everything. He returned to his father's house, and when he went into his father's office, the first thing he saw was that Bible he'd received as a gift many years before. Picking up the Bible, he was remembering what had happened, and as he opened it and began thumbing through the pages, something fell onto the floor; it was a shiny car key. Picking it up, he realized that his father had indeed given him a car many years ago, but he hadn't really opened the gift.

That's what God our Heavenly Father did for us two thousand years ago. A gift wrapped in strips of cloth and placed in a manger. Some have unwrapped that gift, but many are still just looking at the manger scene and never accepting that precious gift of love from God. I opened that gift when I was about twelve years old, and it's been the best gift I've ever received. I accepted that gift of salvation and the promise of eternal life, and my prayer this Christmas is that all of you will open that gift of Jesus. Romans 6:23b says, "But the gift of God is eternal life in Christ Jesus our Lord." (NIV) A gift is not of value until it is opened.

Sitting at my kitchen table has given me many stories to share, and I'm privileged to be able to share this gift of Jesus with all of you. Thanks, dear editor, for this valuable tool of print. I hope we always have a newspaper to read, as I love holding a newspaper in my hands and thumbing through the pages. May you have fun this Christmas unwrapping those gifts you receive and especially the gift of, Jesus.

Letter #32

Forgetting the Past—My Resolution or Goal

December 30, 2017

IT'S A FEW DAYS AFTER CHRISTMAS, AND MY HUS-band, Richard, is in his office working on closing our household books for 2017. He is getting his files ready for the New Year and putting all the records of the old year in boxes to be stored. Richard is organized and likes to have his "books" ready to go when 2018 arrives. What about all of you? Are you ready for the New Year? And what about me? Am I ready for the New Year?

To answer my question, yes, I really think I'm ready for 2018. Thinking about the New Year calendar and those 365 days with nothing written on them, I'm happy that God has given me another year to be with Him on this great earth. Of course, we all yearn for heaven, but being human, we hold onto that golden thread of life with our whole being. I know that someday I will be with Him in heaven because I've accepted Him into my life and love Him with all my heart. I can put the past year behind me and look ahead to the future, perhaps with some regrets but with hope in what God has for my future. In the Bible, in Philippians 3:13c, it says, "Forgetting the past, and looking forward to what lies ahead." (NIV) No matter what has happened in the past year, when I confess my failures and sins, God forgives me and gives me a fresh start.

So what are my resolutions for this coming year? Or should I say, what is my goal? I would like to read my Bible more and have a better prayer life. I would like good health, to be able to walk without pain, to be thankful, to be more loving, and to be more forgiving. In other words, be more like Christ in all I do or say. That is my goal!

And for all of you, I wish you the very best for 2018. May we as a nation be free and have a love for our country and for our fellow man. And may God give you peace and contentment, regardless of what the New Year has in store for you. And may you have companionship with God as you travel these next 365 days. And please remember, I'll be writing again to you and praying for all of you too, right here at my kitchen table, in 2018.

Letter #33
Life Can Be Complex and "Remote"

January 23, 2018

ONCE AGAIN I THANK YOU FOR LETTING ME WRITE letters from my kitchen table and that you are willing to print them. I enjoy sharing some of the events in my life with your readers, and many of them have let me know how much they enjoy my "kitchen table" letters, and for that I'm thankful.

I'm remembering when we got our first TV back in 1951. We had only been married for four years, were busy farming on shares, had no money to spare, and my husband figured that as long as we couldn't afford to go out, we might as well have a TV. Our previous neighbor had one, which was only a six-inch screen, and we had loved watching that. After purchasing our TV, we thought we had died and gone to heaven, as our TV had a whopping fifteen-inch screen, black-and-white picture, and we could turn it on and watch anytime. We turned it on with a knob right below the screen, which was also the volume control, and the channel control was right next to that. These were the only two knobs needed, and we did so enjoy the privilege of owning our own TV with no extra cost.

We now have three televisions, and each one has its own remote control. And the odd part about the remote control is that it has sixty-three buttons that can do mega things if you know which button to push; but it took me three days to learn how to turn it on. First you use the button labeled ON/OFF, with SYSTEM printed above, and you'd think that should do it, but no, you have to quickly press the button labeled TV and the button above that labeled POWER. I'm not very electronically smart, but I think that is a few too many buttons to push to get it up and running. And perish the thought that I should forget to aim it in the right direction, as "no signal" would come on the screen and I would have to start all over again. Also, to make matters worse, we now pay mega bucks to get the programs we want to watch. Whatever happened to free TV?

That got me to thinking that there is still one thing that is free, and that is the love of God. It doesn't cost us a cent, but it cost Jesus His life. Yes, Jesus paid the price for our sins by dying on the cross and rising again on the third day, and He is now in heaven sitting at the right hand of God, ready to welcome us into the family. John 3:16 says, "For God so loved the world that he gave his one and only Son, that whoever believes in him, shall not perish but have eternal life."(NIV) There are no buttons to push and no knobs to turn when you accept that free gift of Jesus' love; simply confess your sins, ask for forgiveness, and accept Him into your heart.

Guess there's not much I can do about the remote, with all its buttons, but maybe someday I'll know what all those buttons are for. If not, I'll wait until my great-grandchildren come to visit, and they'll show me how to make it work. In the meantime, I'll be happy that I have Jesus as my Savior, a warm house to live in, food to eat, and a TV to watch, right here at my kitchen table.

Letter #34

Give Love, Not Gifts, in February

February 8, 2018

CAN'T BELIEVE IT'S ALREADY FEBRUARY, THAT SPEcial time of the year when we celebrate Valentine's Day. I remember when I was in school and received those beautiful little valentines from friends and classmates, and how very excited I was to receive them as well as give them. Now that I'm older, it's not really necessary that I get a card or a box of candy or flowers, as I receive that gift of love from my husband, family, and friends by the many acts of kindness they show me, which gives me the feeling of being loved. I don't need gifts that cost money, as the gift of one's self can show love in other ways, such as helping with the dishes, folding the laundry, a gentle touch, or a goodbye kiss. Now that says, "I love you."

There is a sonnet written in 1850 by Emily Barrett Browning that starts with these words: "How do I love thee, let me count the ways," and goes on to tell in fourteen lines the many ways she feels her love for her husband. It's a beautiful poem written in the old English of that period and not anything like the language of today. She loves without wanting any reward for loving and states that she wishes to be with him all the time, and she ends by saying, "I shall love thee better after death." I too feel the same way about the one I love, after being with him for sixty-nine years; I love him more each day. I love him for the little things that show his love for me and because he also tells me that he loves me, which means a lot.

The Apostle Paul wrote in 1 Corinthians 13:8, "Love never fails." And that is so true, especially where Jesus is concerned. The love of Jesus never ends; even if we don't love Him, He still loves us. Jesus may not love the things we do, but He still loves the person. Paul finishes that chapter with these words in 1 Corinthians 13:13: "And now these three remain: Faith, Hope and Love, these three, but the greatest of these is Love."(NIV)

So as I sit at my kitchen table, let me wish you all a wonderful Valentine's Day and end with these three little words: Jesus loves you.

Letter #35

Prayers for Shootings; Back to Simpler Times

February 20, 2018

THIS LETTER FROM MY KITCHEN TABLE IS A HARD one to write because my heart is filled with sadness, as I've been watching the news about the shootings in Florida. The newspapers and airways are filled with this horrifying news, and we are all shouting, "How could this happen here in America?" Also, my heart is asking, "What has happened to our society that our schools are no longer safe for our children to attend?" I only wish I knew the answer to that. And I'm sure those in authority are anxious to find a way to deal with such horrifying happenings. No child should be afraid to leave the safety of home and go to school, where there is danger, and no parents should be concerned about the safety of their child's life when they are away from home.

In my day life seemed simpler, at least where I lived—on a three-hundred-acre farm situated on a dirt road with very little traffic. We were a large family—I was the tenth child of thirteen—and we didn't go out much, except to church and church doings. For my first three years of school, I attended a little white school house on Alleghany Road, in the small hamlet of Indian Falls. I walked home from school, which was about two miles, and our folks didn't worry about us. I was only six years old when I walked home with Norman, my neighbor, who was five. We got out earlier than our older siblings, and we walked those dirt roads unafraid.

The United States' involvement in the Second World War began in December 1941, and I was only eleven. I think that was the first time I felt fear. We started having air-raid drills in school where we hid under our desks and later went down to the school basement for safety. We had blackouts at night, where we pulled all the shades and only had kerosene lamps for light for about an hour or so. It was all very scary.

Those years have gone, and I'm no longer a kid. With the passing of time, the headlines in the newspapers keep telling of tornados, floods, hurricanes, and shootings—where bad things happen over and over again. Fear seems to be the way we choose to live, and yet while reading my Bible, I came across this verse in Isaiah 41:10: "So do not fear, for I am with you; do not be dismayed, for I am your God. I will strengthen you and help you; I will uphold you with my righteous right hand." (NIV) Maybe if America would allow God back into our schools, and if we turn to Him in prayer, we just might be able to find a way out of our fears and problems. Please, join me as I sit at my kitchen table and lift my heart in prayer, asking that America get back to that "simpler way" of life and let God do the rest.

Letter #36

What Draws Us Back to Our Roots?

March 11, 2018

WELL, I HAVEN'T BEEN SITTING AT MY KITCHEN table for eight days because we took a fast trip to Arizona to visit my sister Ellen. It was a great trip, and I loved being with Ellen and her husband, Jim, for those few days, as we reminisced and laughed about things that happened while we were kids growing up. Since we were so close to California, we also made the six-hour drive to Santa Barbara to visit my sister-in-law Ruth Klotzbach, who will be ninety-nine in April. What a great time we had with all those loved ones, catching up on all the news of the different families and then returning to Sun City for a couple days before heading for home.

It was *good* getting away for a few days, but it was *better* coming back home. What is it that draws us back to our roots, to that safe place with its familiar sounds and warmth, where we feel secure? Yes, we did have a wonderful trip. The weather was great, the plane ride was enjoyable, visiting family was fun, but the thought of going home was always in the back of my mind. And that brings me to the thought of going home to the *best* home of all, to my home in heaven. When I accepted Christ as my Savior, that gave me the key to this heavenly home. Because of Christ shedding His blood on the cross and being resurrected on the third day, He made it possible for all who believe in Him to be with Him in heaven someday. John 3:16 says, "For God so loved the world that he gave his one and only Son, that whoever believes in him should not perish, but have eternal life."(*NIV*) That means a home in heaven, which is forever and the *best*.

Yes, heaven will be the *best* home going of all, and I look forward to that, but not just yet. I have a lot more living to do here on earth—more stories to write, more sermons to preach, maybe I'll even write a book—and lots of wonderful things I want to do until God calls me home to heaven—right here from my kitchen table.

Letter #37

Giving Thanks: Stranger Pays for Milestone Meal

March 24, 2018

W HEN THIS HAPPENED, I WASN'T SITTING AT MY kitchen table, as I was sitting at a table at the Red Lobster restaurant on Transit Road in Williamsville, New York, celebrating my husband Richard's ninety-third birthday. Richard wanted to really have a once-in-a-lifetime celebration, and his mouth was watering for surf and turf. I made reservations for 6:00 p.m., and when we arrived, we were immediately seated at a table.

As we looked over the menu and prices, we realized that this was going to be an expensive dinner, but we both decided that we would splurge and get exactly what we had come for. We both love lobster, so forgetting the price, Richard ordered his surf and turf, and I ordered an all-fish platter of lobster, king crab legs, shrimp, and clams. Of course we had coffee, lobster bisque, and special sweet potatoes as our veggie, which was extra. Needless to say, we enjoyed that meal to the fullest, even knowing that the price and the tip would cost us dearly, but it would be worth it.

After finishing our meal and being full to bursting, our waiter, Sean, asked if we wanted dessert. We both said we couldn't eat another bite. Sean then asked if we could stay for a little singing, and we agreed we could. He and three others returned in a few minutes with a hot fudge sundae topped with one small candle and sang "Happy Birthday" to Richard for his ninety-third birthday. Of course, we did manage to finish the sundae, but we kept waiting for our waiter to return with the bill. After several minutes Sean appeared with our bill and, without giving it to us, held it up and said it was paid for. We were at first in shock and asked, "Who did that?" Sean's reply was that someone in the other room had heard the singing and wanted to know whom it was for, and when he explained that it was for a gentleman who was celebrating his ninety-third birthday, that person then offered to pay for our bill, even though they did not know us. Not only had they paid the bill but also the tip. We owed nothing for that wonderful dinner and service. Needless to say we thanked Sean and asked him to thank whoever was so generous and thoughtful.

In gratitude and with thanksgiving, we left the restaurant hoping to catch a glimpse of our benefactor but saw no one who looked even the least bit guilty. All the way home we rejoiced for such a gift of kindness and thanked the Lord for that person who considered us worthy of such a gift.

That gift of giving got me to thinking of another gift: the gift of salvation, paid for by Jesus many years ago. Romans 5: 8 says, "God demonstrates his own love for us in this: While we were still sinners, Christ died for us."(NIV) Our debt of sin was "paid in full" by Jesus when He died on that cross and rose again three days later. Just as our entire bill was paid for at the Red Lobster, Jesus took the bill for our sins and paid it all so that we might have a home in heaven. You too can have a special blessing this Easter time by accepting Jesus' sacrifice, which He did by dying on that cross and paying your debt in full. So from my kitchen table, please join me in giving thanks for such an act of love.

Letter #38

Saw My First Robin; Spring Is Coming

April 11, 2018

I WAS SITTING, GAZING OUT MY KITCHEN WINDOW, when I saw this little red-breasted bird hopping along in the snow, most likely looking for something to eat, or perhaps looking for scraps of materials that would help to build a nest. The ground was covered with beautiful white snow, and it was cold out, so I was feeling sorry for the little guy, when he gave one last hop and flew off to better territory. He doesn't realize that here in western New York, it is still winter, even though the calendar says it's spring. But seeing my first robin gives me hope that spring is just around the corner.

Now, on Facebook it seems that everyone is complaining how much they hate these spring snow storms and wish that spring would come and how very tired they are of winter. I know we've had a long, cold winter, but actually this beautiful white snow doesn't bother me, as it doesn't stay long and is usually gone by 11:00 a.m. So I'm not complaining, because when it covers the muddy ground, it makes a beautiful, pristine-looking countryside for me to enjoy. Of course I don't have to be out in it, so that might be the reason, and I can't do anything about the weather anyways.

My father-in-law, Frederick Rudolph, used to say, "Spring snows are the poor man's fertilizer." What he meant was that that the spring snows have nitrogen in them and are valuable in making the farmer's crops grow. The ground at this time of year is not frozen, so the snow that falls now will seep into the soil slowly, and with all that nitrogen, it acts like a fertilizer for the farmers. Looked it up on Google, and it's true.

In the Bible, in Acts 1:7, it says, "It is not for you to know the times or the seasons, which the Father has put into his own power." (KJV) This means that God is in control, and He sets the time for winter to go and spring to come. So I'll sit at my kitchen table and watch the seasons come and go, in God's timing, of course.

Letter #39
God Plans Every Thing

April 27, 2018

TODAY IS MY SISTER KATHRYN'S BIRTHDAY. SHE IS six and a half years younger than I am, and as I sit at my kitchen table and look out the window, at this beautiful spring morning, I'm reminded of the day she was born. I was in grade school at the one-room schoolhouse in Indian Falls when Kathryn came into this world. When my siblings and I returned home from school, there, in a large wicker baby buggy, was this tiny eight-pound baby girl, sound asleep. It was a big surprise for us younger ones, as nobody had announced earlier that we would soon have baby number twelve joining the family. That was April 27, 1937, and in those days they didn't announce to young children that someone was pregnant or in the family way, or any other news that might be considered private. Kathryn was accepted and loved, no questions asked, and I don't ever remember being jealous or feeling bad that I hadn't known. I think that life was simpler then—you lived from day to day and didn't concern yourself about tomorrow. Actually God plans everything and knows what each day will bring. We never know what is going to happen from one day to the next, and I for one am content to let God do all the planning. I think it is better that I don't know; that way I don't have to worry.

When I got married, I had no idea that Richard and I would live long enough to be together for sixty-nine years, or that we would have four children. I didn't think about the future. I knew I would have to grow old. I didn't realize that someday it would be hard for me to walk and get around, that my legs and joints would hurt, and I'd have pain and look old and bent. It's not what I would choose, but it's what God has chosen for me. He is teaching me patience, kindness, compassion for others, and to be thankful, but most of all to trust Him, to accept Jesus' salvation into my life and have faith in His plans for me. In the Bible, in James 4:14, it says, "Why, you do not even know what will happen tomorrow. What is your life? You are a mist that appears for a little while and then vanishes." (NIV) God is the one who rules our lives; the world and all of us must learn to accept that fact. I'm trusting God to direct my days, and if I'm granted more time on this earth, I'd like to continue to sit at my kitchen table and reminisce with all of you in my letters to the editor.

Letter #40

Keep the Farmers in Your Prayers

May 17, 2018

THIS IS THE TIME OF YEAR WHEN EVERYTHING IS springing into new life. It's that time of the year for farmers, and for those of you who enjoy planting gardens and working the soil, to begin planting those seeds for a new crop. I really admire those people, as they love working in God's great outdoors. I used to love doing the garden work of trimming the bushes, pulling the weeds, and mowing the lawn, but now I'm not able to get down on my knees or bend over, as I might fall.

Farming is such hard work, and it's never finished. First the soil has to be plowed and fitted to make it ready for planting, which is going over the fields with equipment that breaks up the soil. Then the farmer needs equipment to plant the seeds, which is another time to go over the field to distribute the seeds. The farmer sometimes goes back and forth over a field five or six times, to prepare it for planting if he wants a good crop at harvest time. All this costs money, time, and patience. Then he waits to see if the rains come at the right time and if he'll make any money for all his hard labor. It's a gamble each and every day, hoping and praying for the best. We should be so thankful that we have men and women who love this way of life and are willing to take the chances even when they don't get paid that much for their labor. I know because we once farmed a small farm, and the going was rough. That old saying "You can take the boy out of the farm, but you can't take the farm out of the boy" is so very true. Once born into farming, it remains forever in your heart, even if you make a living in another way.

All this reminds me of a scripture in the Bible that refers to a person who sows the seeds of salvation. Galatians 6:9 says, "Let us not become weary in doing good, for at the proper time we will reap a harvest if we do not give up."(NIV) And that is what life for me is all about—being His for all eternity. Sometimes the work is difficult, but the harvest is worth the effort of preparing the soil of the heart, planting the seeds of righteousness, and reaping a harvest of believers. And I can do that right here from my kitchen table.

Letter #41

A Father Like Mine

June 10, 2018

I'M SITTING AT MY KITCHEN TABLE READING A PAM-phlet that I received in the mail. One profound sentence caught my attention. The sentence went like this: "It's easier to become a father than it is to be a father." How true, I thought as I mulled those words over and over in my mind. Then I realized that I was one of the fortunate ones to have had a father who loved his children, took care of them, and truly was a father.

My dad, Peter Klotzbach Jr., was one of nine children. They were taught at a young age that work was important and nec-essary in order to live and provide for one's family. My dad married my mom, Clara Newkirk, in 1913, and they raised all thirteen of us children with love, discipline, faith in God, and a responsibility to work hard for one's family. My dad was truly a wonderful father.

I called him Dad, and he was one of the godliest men I've ever known. He was a farmer by trade and worked hard and long hours to provide for us, but on Sundays he also preached at a small church in Pembroke. At night time Dad would put us to bed and tell us Bible stories, and he told them so excitingly, we were always ready to go to bed. Dad also had family devotions with all of the family every morning after breakfast, where we all knelt by our chairs and Dad would pray. He always had time for us, and I remember when he preached, it was a simple message that spoke of a God who loved us like a father and a God who would forgive our sins if we asked, and if we accepted Him into our hearts, we would have a home in heaven.

My heart aches for those of you who never had a father like mine. But no matter how bad your dad was or is, you have a Heavenly Father who loves you and who is willing to talk with you anytime, day or night. He is there for you and is waiting for you to call on Him. In Psalm 68:5 it says, "A Father to the fatherless, a defender of widows, is God in his holy dwelling."(NIV) Now, that is a father you can count on.

I still remember my dad and what a blessing it was to have him in my life, and I'm grateful to my Heavenly Father for His blessing of a father like mine. So as I sit at my kitchen table, I'll bow my head and pray for fathers everywhere to be true fathers like mine.

Letter #42

I Graduated Seventy Years Ago

June 19, 2018

SITTING AT MY KITCHEN TABLE READING AN INVI-
tation to another graduation party brings back memories of
when I graduated from Corfu High School on June 28, 1948.
And I'm thinking about how excited I was on that Monday
night many years ago. I can even remember the yellow dress I
wore under my robe, and how thrilled I was that my boyfriend,
Richard, would be there to watch me graduate, as would my
parents and some of my brothers and sisters. I was only seventeen, but I felt so grown-up, and on that graduation day, I was
ready for whatever life would bring.

Then I blinked my eyes, and when I opened them, I realized that those years had passed ever so quickly. I was married, had children, and celebrated graduations with them and
marriages. Worked at different jobs, welcomed grandchildren
and great-grandchildren, and now I'm asking, "Where did all
those years go? How can this be? It was only yesterday I graduated." No, time galloped by when I wasn't looking, and now

my classmates and I are in the process of planning and looking forward to our seventieth graduation celebration.

If I could give advice to those who are graduating this year, I'd tell them to face life with great eagerness. Don't expect something for nothing. Work hard and don't rely on things of this world to bring you happiness; let God direct your path with His love and grace.

In the Bible, in James 4:14–15, it says, "Why, you do not even know what will happen tomorrow. What is your life? You are a mist that appears for a little while and then vanishes. Instead, you ought to say, if it is the Lord's will, we will live and do this or that."(NIV) So trust Him with your future. I didn't know what life had in store for me, seventy years ago, but I do thank God, that I had Jesus in my life and trusted Him to do the leading, all I had to do was follow.

In the meantime, I'm happy to be invited to three graduation parties, and I'm asking God to bless those graduates, as they face their future with hope, faith, and trust. My job is to pray for all those who are graduating in 2018, and I can do that right here at "my Kitchen Table."

Jean's graduation picture, 1948

Letter #43

Sitting at Don's Museum

June 29, 2018

YOU COULD NEVER GUESS WHERE I WAS SITTING ON Saturday, June 23, as it was twenty miles from my kitchen table. My husband, Richard, and I were sitting at my brother-in-law Don's home, at his Farm Museum Building directly behind his house. This farm museum, full of machinery, buggies, wagons, tools, and other articles pertaining to farming, was being opened to the public for this one day to coincide with the Agricultural Days celebration in Bennington, New York. Don couldn't be there, as he was out of town, so he asked Richard if he would be able to fill in for him, and of course Richard was happy to oblige, and I wanted to go along, as I didn't want to miss out on all the fun.

This museum, featuring Rudolph farm antiques, is very special. My sister-in-law Jean Marie was the one who had the idea for a museum. She was a music teacher at Alexander Central School for many years, and when she retired, this dream became a reality. She had been collecting many antique articles of farming through the years as well as things from her side of the family. Her parents, Violet and Clarence Dab, had an old-time grocery store in West Seneca for many years, and Jean had lots of memorable items from that store that she had saved, and she needed a place to display them. Don had a barn built so Jean could use it for her museum. Jean's museum is about forty feet by twenty-four feet and full of all sorts of information on farm life and days of yester year. There are farm tools and machinery from the Rudolph side and antique items from the Dabb family store. Jean Marie has displayed these priceless pieces of history from bygone days, and it's a joy to show them to others and relive the life of what farming used to be like.

Our ancestors worked hard, and the rewards were not always of material value; their lives were centered on family and on God. The life of a farmer is not an easy life, but working with nature brings one closer to our Creator, as you depend on Him for everything—the weather, your health, your livelihood, and life itself. In the Bible, in 1 Corinthians 3:7–8, it says, "So neither he who plants nor he who waters is anything, but only God, who makes things grow. The man who plants and the man who waters have one purpose, and each will be rewarded according to his own labor."(NIV) This is speaking of planting the Word of God and those who help that seed to grow by watering with prayers and telling others about the love of Jesus. As Christians we need to be planting seeds of God's love wherever we go. Just as farmers rely on God for His rain and sun for their crops to grow, we too need to rely on God's love to produce a crop for Him. God is there with us, loving us, caring for us, and ready to harvest that final crop for His kingdom, and I can water those planted seeds with prayer right here at my kitchen table.

Letter #44

I'll Take a Call from God but Not Those Pesky Telemarketers

July 24, 2018

I JUST GOT ANOTHER ONE OF THOSE ANNOYING calls from a telemarketer on my cell phone, informing me that she could help me with my student loans. That made me laugh, as I didn't attend college, and besides, I'm now eighty-seven years old. When I told her I wasn't interested, she kept right on talking, and I couldn't get a word in edgewise. I decided that the only way to stop the call was to hang up, which I did. I usually don't answer my cell phone unless it's a 585 number, but this one was. I don't know all the numbers of my grandchildren, so I decided to answer the call, which proved to be a big mistake! I think it's very intrusive when it's my landline home phone, but when it's my cell, that's off-limits. I don't have a smart phone, but I carry my flip one with me everywhere I go, just in case I need it, as it's comforting to know I can call for help anytime. My cell phone is for my safety and convenience, not for telemarketers. What can I do? Not much; just accept things as they are!

It's a good thing God accepts us as we are and loves us anyway. Unlike us, God loves to hear from us anytime, anyplace. He waits for us to call Him through prayer and is anxious to hear from us morning, noon, or night. We don't have to have a special time or number, as we have a direct line to our Heavenly Father through prayer. In the Bible, in 1 Thessalonians 5:16–18, it tells us to "Be joyful always; pray continually; give thanks in all circumstances, for this is God's will for you in Christ Jesus."(NIV) Just as I have my phone for comfort and safety, I have prayer that is there for me in the same way. Sometimes God speaks to me in different ways to let me know He's there, waiting to hear from me. Of course it's not audible, but somehow I get a gentle nudge to stop and offer a quick prayer.

As the preceding scripture says, pray continually, and be thankful. What a way to start the day, and I can do that through prayer right here at my kitchen table.

Letter #45

My Seventieth Class Reunion of Corfu High School

August 30, 2018

WELL, I WENT TO MY SEVENTIETH CORFU HIGH School alumni luncheon on August 4, 2018, at Denny's Restaurant at the Flying J, and I had a great time. We enjoyed our lunch and sat around and reminisced for about an hour or more.

Of course we all looked much older than we did seventy years ago, and not very many were able to attend. There were only eight class members, but with our spouses and friends, we did have thirteen in attendance.

We read letters sent by those unable to attend, reported on phone calls we received, and out of the forty-six original members, we realized that twenty-seven of our class members are now deceased, two we don't know where they are, and only seventeen members are living. Those living out of state and unable to travel so far made for the low attendance.

For me, this was so much fun! But talking to others, even some of my own family, they can't see why we think it is so important to get together with alumni friends. One friend asked me why I thought it necessary to renew old times and see friends of years ago, why was that important to me? Actually, I really didn't have an answer. I guess it's traveling back in time to feel young again, to relive those school days that I enjoyed so much, and to thank God for life and friends from childhood days. To be happy and share with others that life has been good to me, and that I'm blessed to be alive and to share my life with my schoolmates.

Maybe it's reliving past days again and knowing how fortunate I am to have lived when I did, to appreciate what I had and rejoice in what I now have. In Ecclesiastes 3:1 it says, "There is a time for everything, and a season for every activity under heaven."(NIV)

Yes, there is a time to reminisce and a season for us to have an alumni celebration. I think God wants us to have a good time here on earth until He calls us home.

And as long as I can write letters to the editor and commune with people in this way, I'll just sit at my kitchen table and reminisce with the friends I've made through my letters.

Letter #46
From My Kitchen Table:
Learning and Serving

September 5, 2018

As I woke at 6:30 this morning and got out of bed, I realized that today school would be starting. Our dear children would be returning to school to start another year of learning, and I began thinking, "Do I still remember some of the things I learned in school, such as the multiplication tables?" As I went to the kitchen to start my day, I began to mull them over in my mind, starting with eight times one, and why I started with those, I don't know, but those numbers flashed through my mind from one to twelve, and I remembered each one. Of course I gave myself a pat on the back for remembering, as at my age that is a really good sign that I'm still with it mentally; at least I hope so.

Then I wondered if, in today's educational system, children have to learn the multiplication tables, or is that obsolete? So much of what we had to learn is no longer necessary with today's electronics and computer know how, but I think the children of today need some of the basics we learned, such as the times tables, cursive writing, regular math, English, more about history, and even geography.

Then I began to think about the story of King Solomon in the Bible, where he was asked what he wanted from God. Solomon didn't ask God to give him power or money or fame or health but wisdom. In today's world we want all those things and more. Education is promised to everyone by our government, but wisdom only comes from God. In James 1:5 it says, "If any of you lacks wisdom, he should ask God, who gives generously to all without finding fault, and it will be given to him."(NIV) Do we ask for that, or do we feel we are getting everything we need through our educational system and we can get along fine without God? Big mistake; we all need wisdom that only God can give.

Another verse, Proverbs 15:14, says, "The discerning heart seeks knowledge, but the mouth of a fool feeds on folly."(NIV) So much of what is on TV, on our computers, and what we read, is not good for us. Do we still feed on that trash, or do we look for the more nourishing food of knowledge and become wise by listening to God and reading the Bible, which is full of the Good News and the wisdom we all long for?

That's why I'm going to sit at my kitchen table and look into God's Word each and every day and ask God for wisdom that I might serve Him better until He calls me home.

Letter #47

Looking Back to Our Wedding Day

October 8, 2018

I AWOKE WITH THE WORDS OF A SONG GOING through my mind. It was the one that was sung at our wedding on October 22, 1948.

The song was "I Love You Truly," which was very popular in my time. The first verse wasn't the one going through my mind. It was the third verse that was not originally included but was added later, and the words went something like this: "We love each other, truly dear, but there is Another whom we hold more dear. Take thou our lives on this our wedding day, use them for Thyself Lord, this we pray." And we did just that, accepting the Lord as the third partner in our marriage on that day. I remember it well; we pledged our love to each other, and we never looked back. We were young, and the future looked good.

Those seventy years have passed all too quickly, and I don't know where the time has gone. Of course those years had their ups and downs, but we managed to weather them all, and our love is still there because we had the Lord to help us as we traveled the roads of married life with him. I'm so very thankful that God chose my husband, Richard, for me many years ago, and I do believe that God was wise in His choice.

That's what God had in mind thousands of years ago when He placed Adam in the Garden of Eden, and realizing that Adam was lonely without a help mate, God created Eve from one of Adam's ribs, and that was the beginning of what we today call marriage. In Genesis 2:24 it says, "For this reason a man will leave his father and mother and be united to his wife, and they will become one flesh."(NIV) What a promise from God, to become one. Those years have brought much happiness, and though we may not be considered wealthy in terms of money and possessions, we are blessed with many treasures: our four children and their mates, our ten grandchildren and their mates, and our twenty-four great-grandchildren, plus many other wonderful relatives, loved ones, and friends.

Richard and I are looking forward to the celebrations we are having planned by our children—Mona, Betty, Ken, and Tracy—and their spouses. They are honoring us at a family banquet on Saturday with our family of fifty-three, and then on Sunday, October 28, with a Dessert Open House at the Indian Falls United Methodist Church from 2:00 p.m. until 5:00 p.m. What an honor to be celebrated in this way by our children, and I'm looking forward to giving up my place at my kitchen table and sitting for a few hours at our special party. And someday I will have a special place at another table in heaven, when He calls me home.

"Our Wedding Day"

"Jean and Richard on their 70th Anniversary"

Letter #48
My Thanksgiving Cup Runneth Over
November 20, 2018

IT'S RATHER LATE TO GET A LETTER IN THE PAPER before Thanksgiving, but I really think that I have to say something about one of the most important holidays of the year. Now, believe me it is no problem finding something to write about, as I have so much to be thankful for.

Reading the letter that was in Monday's paper from the gentleman Paul Trowbridge, who writes from his "View from the Tractor Seat," reminded me of so many things, from my childhood days and through the years, that I also have to be thankful for. As he stated in his article, they "never lacked for anything." Even though they were a poor farm family, they didn't know they were poor.

I was raised in the same way, so I don't recall not having some of the finer things of life. Hand-me-downs were some of the things we cherished the most, because they were from our older siblings. My mom did a lot of sewing and making of our clothes, so I always felt I had the best. We didn't know we were poor money wise because of all the love they showered on us. Life was simple, and we were thankful for each other.

There is a song titled "Aren't You Glad You're You?" One part of the songs says, and I quote, "And when you wake up each morn, aren't you glad that you were born. Think what you've got the whole day through, aren't you glad you're you?" Yes, I truly am happy to be me. That I had the parents I had, that I live in America, and that I came from a family of thirteen children. That I married Richard, that my children love me, that I have lots of grand-children and lots of friends, that I can go to church and worship as I choose, and that God made me who I am.

In Psalm 139:13–14 it says, "For you created my inmost being; you knit me together in my mother's womb. I praise you because I am fearfully and wonderfully made; your works are wonderful, I know that full well."(NIV)

So this Thanksgiving Day I'm going to be glad that I'm alive and that I'm who I am. And I'll be thankful I'm able to sit at my kitchen table, have a cup of coffee, and reminisce about those past precious days of long ago, and that I have the privilege of writing letters to the *Daily News* and that they publish them.

Letter #49

Open the Gift of Jesus This Year

December 10, 2018

I AWOKE EARLY THIS MORNING AND COULDN'T GET back to sleep, as I kept thinking about what I wanted to write for my Christmas letter to the *Daily News*. I got up, and instead of going to my kitchen table, I proceeded to my computer to write down my thoughts about Christmas.

I wondered, "Why do we give gifts for Christmas, and when did that start? How about shopping to find the perfect gift, and then, instead of signing my name to that gift, I give the credit to Santa Claus? How did that happen?" I guess it more or less evolved, little by little down through the years to shape the celebration of what we now call Christmas.

I know Christmas was started thousands of years ago, when that tiny baby boy, Jesus, was wrapped in swaddling clothes and laid in a manger. It says in Luke 2:7, "And she gave birth to her firstborn, a son. She wrapped Him in cloths and placed Him in a manger, because there was no room for them in the Inn."(NIV) Yes, God gave the first gift, the precious gift of

Jesus, to a sin-sick world. The shepherds were the first to receive that gift from God, and they went and told others. Now it's our job to tell others of this gift of Jesus that we celebrate at Christmas time.

Thankfully, I opened that gift many years ago, when I was twelve years of age. I have treasured that gift because I opened it and have accepted Jesus' love and sacrifice into my heart. But if I had never opened or used that gift, it would be of no use to me. Yes, God sent His gift of Jesus thousands of years ago, but some have never opened that gift. What good is a gift if it is never opened or used?

I'm sure when you receive your gifts this year from under the Christmas tree, you will open them and whatever you receive, you will put to good use. So I'm hoping that you too will open the gift of Jesus, which God gave the world so many centuries ago, and find out what a difference that gift will make in your life. And from my kitchen table, let me wish you a very Merry Christmas!

Letter #50

Don't Throw Jesus Away
like the Tree after Christmas

January 1, 2019

THE BUSY MONTH OF DECEMBER IS OVER, AND NOW I can turn my calendar over to the month of January and to a brand-new year. We had a great Christmas, and it seems like we celebrated it all month long, starting with our big Rudolph family celebration on December 6. That's the one we call the Frederick and Mildred Rudolph Get-Together.

This includes our family members and also Richard's brother and sister and all their family members, which if all of them came there would be around 105 people. This year we were fortunate to have more than fifty-five there, and we held it at a church in Akron. A great time of fellowship, food, reminiscing, games, and fun was enjoyed by all. Then we had another Christmas get-together of about twenty-five on December 16 at church, with some of the members of our immediate family who couldn't be with us on Christmas Eve.

Then on Christmas Eve, after attending our church service, we celebrated again with the giving of gifts, food, and fun with about fifteen others of our family.

Those in North Carolina couldn't make it this year for Christmas, so we sent them their gifts. Then on December 28 we had the Klotzbach family Christmas at the Indian Falls Fire Hall, which is my side of our family, but only a small number of about thirty-five were able to attend. Just how blessed can one be to celebrate the birth of Jesus all month long? And with the New Year coming, we won't stop celebrating Jesus, as He is a big part of our lives. Just because Christmas is past doesn't mean it's over. No, Jesus is alive in our hearts and in our home to be worshipped and honored and thanked all year long.

My prayer is that you too will keep the gift of Jesus with you in this New Year of 2019 and make Him a part of your life as you serve Him, worship Him, and tell others of His love and grace. In 1 John 4:15 it says, "If anyone acknowledges that Jesus is the Son of God, God lives in him and he in God."(NIV) So don't throw Jesus away with the tree or put Him in the attic with the other decorations. Take Him with you during 2019. Let Him dwell in you and make this a year of peace, happiness, love, and faith, and I'll join with you in doing the same, right here at my kitchen table.

Letter #51

The Pains of Life and Age
Healed by the Good Book

January 30, 2019

I GOT UP EARLY THIS MORNING, AS MY LEGS HURT me so much that I couldn't get back to sleep. My neuropathy and arthritis were making my feet burn and my legs and knees hurt and ache. I didn't want to wake Richard, so I went to the kitchen and sat down at my kitchen table to read. Picking up my Bible, I scanned the pages, looking for some comforting Scripture that would help me to forget the aches and pains in my body. I needed an early-morning time with Jesus to thank Him for giving me a good night's rest and waking me to another day.

I think we forget to thank Him for the important things in life, those everyday happenings that we take for granted, such as waking up to enjoy another day here on earth, for every breath we take, being able to eat and take nourishment, going to the bathroom, all those everyday things that we do automatically when we open our eyes to a new day.

I've had trouble with my knees and legs for some time now, and I know that my age has a lot to do with it, but I don't want to give up and not try to help myself. I try to stay busy with housework, getting meals, doing the washing, and reading, so it's not that I don't get a little exercise. I've gone on Google and found out a little about neuropathy, and there is not much one can do, as there is no cure. I don't have diabetes, which usually causes neuropathy, so I'm thankful for that. But I do have trouble standing up straight when I walk, and that is what bothers me, as I look like an old lady, which I am, but I don't want to look old. That's my pride kicking into gear; the dictionary says that pride is conceit, self-respect, haughty behavior, disdain, and I don't want to be like that either.

Now what does the Bible say about pride? Well, if you look at Proverbs 16:18, it says, "Pride goes before destruction, a haughty spirit before a fall."(NIV) Then, I guess I better change, as I don't want to fall, and I don't want to become conceited and think I'm too good to get old and bent over. So if that is my lot in life, I guess I better accept it. I'm still standing and still walking, so no matter what, I'm going to enjoy being me. No matter how I look, as long as I look to Jesus for His strength and care, I'll be content in the way that I look and walk. I'll sit at my kitchen table, have my second cup of coffee, read my Bible, have a time of prayer, and be content to rest in God's love.

Letter #52
God's Special Valentine

February 11, 2019

As I looked at the calendar today, I realized that Valentine's Day is almost here, and that got me to reminiscing about my courting days when Richard and I were dating. We'd only been dating about two months when that romantic day of February 14th arrived. Richard and I had a date that night, and when he came to pick me up, he handed me a beautiful red, heart-shaped box of candy with a pretty card attached. Now for me that was like Christmas all over again. I'd never, ever received boxed candy before, and this was one special heart-shaped delicacy just for me. Needless to say I was thrilled, excited, and in love. Now, my younger brother and sisters were as excited as I was and were waiting for me to open it and share it with them, but my selfish nature was saying, "No, it's mine." That didn't last long, and the next day I opened that box and shared it with all of them. But to this day I still treasure that memory and the love that was in that red, heart-shaped box of candy.

This got me to thinking about a Sunday school song associated with Valentine's Day. I remember teaching my Carolers Choir this song many, many years ago. The melody was catchy, and the words spoke of another valentine we all should have. The words went something like this:

"Roses are red, Violets are blue, God sent a Valentine 'specially for you. God sent a Valentine 'specially for you, God sent a Valentine 'specially for you. Isn't it great? Isn't it true? God sent a Valentine 'specially for you."

Yes, God did send us the best valentine of all, His son, Jesus. And Jesus willingly came and gave His life for us that we might have a home in heaven. All we have to do is receive that valentine (Jesus) into our hearts and live for Him, and that assures us of a home in heaven. Now, that is the best valentine anyone can receive.

In 1 John 4:9–10 it says, "This is how God showed his love among us: He sent his one and only Son into the world that we might live through him. This is love: not that we loved God, but that he loved us and sent his Son as an atoning sacrifice for our sins."(NIV) And we can rely on that love. I think that is enough of a gift for me on this Valentine's Day; I don't need flowers or candy. I'll be at my kitchen table having a cup of coffee with Richard and our "Special Valentine."

"Jean and Richard dating 1948"

Letter #53
Why He Gives Us a New Life Each Spring

March 19, 2019

WHILE HAVING LUNCH TODAY, I LOOKED OUT MY kitchen window and noticed that the snow that came last night was melting away into the grassy, green-black soil, and the thought came to me that spring was just around the corner. My heart did a little shout of joy as I thought about the changing of seasons, and I was so happy that I live where we have the different seasons of the year—winter, spring, summer, and fall. It's like having something to look forward to, as each time of year brings something new to life. I remember when winter came and the first snow fall was so exciting, as I looked forward to that time of the year, and now once again I am ready to welcome the newness of spring, when the birds return, the trees sprout leaves, and the new growth makes the earth alive again.

Yes, I'm looking forward to spring and the newness of the earth as it bursts forth into bloom. In the Bible, in Ecclesiastes 3:1, it says, "There is a time for everything, and a season for every activity under heaven."(NIV) God has given us the different seasons to look forward to and enjoy all the wonders each season brings. Spring seems to be the season that wakes up the earth from her slumber, and the beginning of growth springing up from the ground is a promise that life is renewed once again. God is ready to renew the earth and give us a reason to go on. The work of starting new with another season fills our days with the splendor of God's beautiful world.

Another blessing for this time of the year for me is that God has seen fit to let my husband celebrate another birthday soon; he turns ninety-four on Saturday. Richard is also looking forward to being out and clearing off the lawns at home and church to get ready for the mowing. This will mean lots of work but also a blessing, to be outdoors in nature, helping to change something messy and dirty-looking into green grass, budding trees, and blooming flowers. God's handiwork shows us that He loves us. Jesus also offers new life if we accept Him into our hearts. In the Bible, in 2 Corinthians 5:17, it says, "Therefore, if anyone is in Christ, he is a new creation; the old has gone, the new has come!"(NIV) Just as spring brings the blooming of new life, we can spiritually have new life in Christ. So I'm going to enjoy watching spring come right from my kitchen table and know that I too am a new creation, because I've accepted Jesus into my heart.

Letter #54

Why We Celebrate Easter

April 5, 2019

With the beginning of April, my thoughts turned to one of the most spiritual times of the year, Easter, and my heart seemed to sing with the thought of how Jesus died for me so that I might have life everlasting. Those precious holy days before Jesus willing went to die on the cross seemed to come into my mind, and once again I began to live those days from Palm Sunday through Easter Sunday. This is a short version of what took place many years ago on that week we call Holy Week. It started out with such joy and ended with wonder, amazement, a miracle, and those joyous words: "He lives!"

Palm Sunday was just an ordinary day for the disciples and Jesus until they brought a donkey to him. In Mark 11:7–9 (NIV), it tells how they placed Jesus on that animal, and He rode into Jerusalem being proclaimed as king, with people waving palm branches and shouting Hosannas and singing His praises. What a joyous day that was!

Matthew 21:12–13 (NIV) tells us that Monday was different: As Jesus walked toward the temple, He became angry as He noticed the crooked moneychangers selling and cheating the people who came to the temple to worship and bring their sacrifices. In righteous anger Jesus grabbed a whip and began to chase those people out of the temple by over turning their tables and setting livestock free. This was Jesus' way of cleansing the holy temple and letting people know that it is wrong to desecrate God's house of worship.

Then on Tuesday we find Jesus in the temple preaching and teaching all those who were anxious to hear what He had to say. On Wednesday the Bible is silent on what took place, as nothing is written of what happened that day.

Then on Thursday the disciples were told to get a room so that they could celebrate the Passover. The Passover meal was prepared, and then Jesus got up from the table, took off His outer garment and, filling a basin with water, began to wash the disciples' feet. Now, the disciples thought it was strange that Jesus should serve them, and only Peter protested until Jesus said to him, "If I don't wash your feet you have no part with me" (John 13:8, NIV). Of course Peter relented and even suggested that He wash his head also. When Jesus finished washing their feet, they all gathered at the table. While eating the Passover meal, Jesus took bread, gave thanks, and broke it, and gave it to them, saying, "This is my body broken for you; do this in remembrance of me" (Luke 22:19, NIV). Then after supper He took the cup and said, "This is my blood, of the new covenant, which is poured out for you, but the hand of the man who is going to betray me, is with mine on the table" (Luke 22:20–21, NIV). Then Judas left to betray Jesus to the religious leaders.

After supper Jesus went out to the garden with the disciples for a time of prayer. By now it was late, around midnight. Jesus went to pray, and the disciples fell asleep; Jesus returned and woke them. Then Judas was seen coming with a large crowd of soldiers and kissed Jesus, which was the sign to the soldiers that this was indeed Jesus. The soldiers arrested Jesus and took Him to the high priest and then from Caiaphas to Pilate. Peter denied Jesus three times, and the cock crowed. Pilate wanted to let Jesus go free, but the religious leaders asked for Jesus to be crucified.

Early in the morning on Friday, Pilate offered Barabbas in Jesus' place, but they kept shouting for Jesus' death. Once again Jesus was led away and flogged. Then, with a crown of thorns on His head and His body wracked with pain, He walked and stumbled up Golgotha Hill. Carrying His own cross, then hung on that cross, with nails driven into His hands and feet, suffering pain and thirst for hours, He was left to die. It was three in the afternoon when Jesus cried out to God and said, "It is finished!" (John 19:30, NIV) The sky went black, the earth shook, rocks split, and graves broke open and those who had died came to life. When the centurion saw this happening, he was terrified and exclaimed, "Surely he was the Son of God!"(Matt.27:54b, NIV)

As sunset came, two men—Joseph of Arimathea and Nicodemus—took Jesus' body off the cross and buried Him in a tomb. Authorities rolled a large stone in front of the tomb so no one could steal the body of Jesus. The sun was setting, and this was the beginning of the Jewish Sabbath. Saturday morning was quiet; no one was around; they were all in hiding. Nothing is written in the Bible about what happened that day, but I'm sure they were all in shock and feeling sad and defeated.

Sunday broke, and Mary hurried to the tomb and found it empty! She ran to tell the disciples, and Peter and John ran to the tomb. John got there first and looked in; Peter pushed past him and entered the tomb, only to find the burial cloths folded and laying where Jesus' head had been—but no Jesus. They walked away, but Mary stayed and was crying when someone appeared and asked her why she was crying. She said, "Because they have taken my Lord away and I don't know where they have laid Him"(John 20:13, NIV). Then a voice called to her, "Mary," and she turned to him and said, "Teacher" (John 20:16, NIV). Yes, Jesus had risen, just as He said He would. The grave could not hold Him! Jesus conquered death that first Easter morning many thousands of years ago and is still alive today. This Easter, won't you too celebrate His resurrection and accept Him as your Savior. That is what Holy Week is all about!

As I again read these happenings in my Bible, I can rejoice that Jesus was willing to make that sacrifice for my sins that I might have an eternal home in heaven. So rejoice with me this Easter Sunday in praising God in whatever church you may attend. Let me shout it right now from my kitchen table: "Hallelujah, Christ is Risen!"

Letter #55
Honoring Mother

May 2, 2019

I KNOW IT'S BEEN A LONG TIME SINCE I'VE WRITTEN anything from my kitchen table, and I do apologize for that. In church last Sunday a friend asked where my letters were, as they hadn't seen any in the *Daily News* in a long time and had been looking for one. I can't believe that it is already May 2, so almost a month has gone by since I last wrote. I guess it's time I put on my thinking cap and get a letter written.

Since this is the month we honor mothers, I wanted to write something that would be appropriate. I've written a lot about my own mother, Clara Newkirk Klotzbach, and what a great mom she was, so I won't repeat myself in singing her praise. Then I began to wonder who started this day to honor mothers. The credit for this special day is given to Anna Jarvis but was originally started by her mother and other mothers back in 1850 to honor all grieving women and to remember fallen soldiers and work for peace. Her mother died in 1905, and in 1908 Anna Jarvis wanted to honor her mom for all she had done and for being such a great mother. In 1914 President Woodrow Wilson signed a declaration making the second Sunday in May the official date to celebrate Mother's Day. Anna never meant for it to become a commercial event and tried to fight it until her death in 1948, at the age of eighty-four. Today we spend $133 million on Mother's Day cards alone, and on other gifts— such as flowers, candy, and other things—we spend another $20 million, according to the National Retail Federation.

When I was a little girl, my father always bought pink carnation flowers for each of us children in honor of our mother. Pink flowers were for us kids to wear because our mom was alive. The white carnations were for my mom and dad, as their mothers had passed away. I was always grateful that my flower was pink and hoped I'd never have to wear a white carnation.

This got me to thinking about who the first mother was, and that would be Eve, who was mentioned in the Bible in the Book of Genesis. Then while reading about her, I realized that neither Adam nor Eve had a mother. Adam was created by God, from the earth, and Eve was taken from Adam's rib, and God created her, too. Neither one of them was born but created. Eve had the very first baby, a boy named Cain, and since then the miracle of birth has happened over and over. Psalm 139:14 says, "I will praise thee for I am fearfully and wonderfully made; your works are wonderful, I know that full well." (NIV) So on Sunday, May 12, let us celebrate mothers everywhere and thank God for the miracle of birth. Let us also honor those many women who take care of children and love children but have never had the privilege of becoming a mother. And even though my mom is no longer with me, I can still pause and remember what a great mom she was and give thanks for her right here at my kitchen table.

Letter #56

A Call and a Prayer Saved a Heart

May 28, 2019

THE PAST WEEK WAS A BUSY ONE, AS SO MUCH HAS happened. I received news that my baby sister, Ellen, who lives in Arizona, was having a heart problem. She was admitted to the hospital, and they needed prayers. I called Jill Klotzbach, who is in charge of the prayer line for our church, to start calling people to pray. I had no idea how bad Ellen was, but when someone is seventy-nine and a call asking for prayer comes, our church goes into action. I also started to call members of my brothers' and sisters' families. As I've said before, there were thirteen of us children, and all but four of us girls have gone to their heavenly reward. So I tried to call one member of each of the twelve families to call their loved ones and to pray for their Aunt Ellen. Nieces and nephews and sisters and in-laws immediately got to work to spread the news. My daughter put it on our Klotzbach family message page on the computer, and hundreds of people were praying almost immediately. Praise the Lord, our prayers were answered, as Ellen was taken to surgery, where her heart was shocked, and a couple of days later she was home.

This all took place on a Tuesday; she was home by Thursday and went to work on Saturday. We truly have a great God!

That got me to thinking that God is never too busy to listen when we pray. Our prayers don't have to be eloquent with fancy words, just sincere and from the heart. Prayer is having a conversation with God, asking for our wants and needs, all in the name of Jesus. In the Bible, in John 14:14, Jesus says, "You may ask me for anything in my name, and I will do it."(NIV) Yes, He surely did! As family members and friends in western New York and Arizona were praying, and also those people around the world were lifting Ellen up in prayer, Jesus was listening and granting our request for healing. How thankful we were for all those prayers and for doctors and nurses who have the ability to know what to do, and for Jesus' readiness in answering our requests.

We were delighted that Ellen got well, but if God had seen fit to answer our prayers with a no, and would have taken her home to heaven, we would have known that God loved her more and needed her to be with Him. Because of our prayers, God knew how very much she was still needed here on earth and granted our request.

My prayers for all of you who read my letters is that you will rejoice with me over Ellen's healing, that you too have Jesus in your heart, and will use this privilege of prayer every day. Where? Everywhere, and also right here at my kitchen table.

Letter #57

Freedom Is Not Free; Someone Paid the Price

July 3, 2019

I WOULD LIKE TO APOLOGIZE TO ALL OF YOU WHO read my letters, as I have been negligent in writing lately. It's been more than a month since my last letter, and I didn't even write one for the month of June, so I missed out in honoring fathers, and for that I am sorry. Our children and grandchildren did honor their father and grandfather with cards, dinner out, a leaf blower, gift cards, money, candy, and nuts, so Richard was well taken care of. He definitely felt wrapped in love and respect as well.

The reason I want to apologize for not writing is that several of my friends reminded me that they hadn't seen any letter from me in a long time, and each day they have been looking. I tend to procrastinate and put things off to do later, only later never comes. It really is flattering for me that so many people read my letters and also how much they enjoy them. Sitting at my kitchen table is one job I enjoy doing, as it gives me time to think about the reason God has put me on earth. I love people and enjoy connecting with them through my letters and conversing with them about life. I like to remind them that so many times we overlook the small pleasures of life that God has given us to enjoy and are inclined to want more instead of being content with what we have. In Hebrews 13:5 it states: "Keep your lives free from the love of money and be content with what you have, because God said, 'Never will I leave you; never will I forsake you.'"(NIV)

We in America should be content as an example to others because we have so much. Most of us never go to bed hungry or fear for our lives or are afraid to pray and tell others about Jesus. Most of us take our freedoms for granted, never stopping to realize that someone had to pay for that freedom. Our veterans fought and paid the price for the freedoms we enjoy and the privileges we have here in America. Let us remember the price they paid as we once again celebrate the Fourth of July, when America was born back in 1776.

Also, let's remember that Jesus paid the price for our sins by dying on that cross more than two thousand years ago that we might have freedom from sin and death. In John 15:13 Jesus said, "Greater love has no one than this, that he lay down his life for his friend."(NIV) Yes, Jesus willing went to the cross that we might have life with Him in heaven. Let us take a moment to thank all those veterans for the freedoms we enjoy here in America, and let us thank God for Jesus, who paid our sin debt, and we can do that right here at my kitchen table.

Letter #58

Celebrating the Genesee County Fair

July 22, 2019

WHAT A GREAT WEEK IT WAS FOR CELEBRATING THE 180th anniversary of the Genesee County Fair. Of course we had rain, or it wouldn't have been the fair. Rain, hot weather, and fun times just seem to go together, at least at the Batavia, New York, fairgrounds. Nothing seems to dampen the spirits of all the 4H children and all the adults who bring their produce, exhibits, and animals to the fair. The fair may be over, but there are those who are still talking about it and reliving those past fun-filled days. I had several nieces, nephews, cousins, and even a great-granddaughter who brought their prized animals, sewing projects, baked goods, vegetables, and wood projects to exhibit to win prizes. The cattle, sheep, goats, pigs, horses, rabbits, and chickens delighted those who love to pet and see live animals. There were also many stands that furnished food and drinks for sale and also sugary dough treats and of course ice cream.

The rides were fun, and the pig races captured the kids' and adults' attention, as did the farm machinery. The children loved the kids' tractor pull, and the balloon demonstration was fun to watch, as the lady made the many different animals from long, thin balloons to give away. At the main building, there were displays and merchants selling or advertising their wares, which provided a fun walk and time out of the sun. The parade was small and very home town, where the 4H kids decorated floats, marched in the parade, and tossed candy to spectators along the route just to show their love for the fair. The sheriff's dept, firemen, fair queen, veterans, and local political officials marched in support of the fair to help make it a fun time for all. And in the entertainment tent, each day and evening brought many different types of music and fun events to watch and enjoy. Also the grandstand programs were fun and entertaining for those who attended.

I guess you could say that the 180th anniversary of the Genesee County Fair in Batavia, New York, was a huge success and plenty of fun for everyone who attended. There were many faithful volunteers and fair officers who helped plan and produce this special celebration; also the *Daily News* helped with all the pictures and notices of events and happenings they published on the fair. I think we owe them all a vote of thanks for all they did in bringing this fair to life.

In 1 Thessalonians 5:18 it says, "Give thanks in all circumstances, for this is God's Will for you in Christ Jesus." (NIV) Yes, it never hurts to give thanks for all those things we enjoy here on this earth. So let me say a big thank-you to all those who helped to make this particular 2019 fair a great time for everyone, and I can do that right here from my kitchen table.

Letter #59

Navigating the Blind Spot in Life from My Kitchen Table

August 8, 2019

TODAY I WAS TRAVELING DOWN THE ROAD WHERE I live, and when I reached Wyman Road, a car was coming out to turn onto Akron Road. He slowly inched his way out until he was almost in my lane of traffic because that is a blind corner. When you turn from Wyman onto Akron, you can't see what is coming from the west until you are almost on Akron Road because of the trees and weeds on the roadside. Now, that is a bad corner, but that doesn't compare to the turn at the end of Akron Road proceeding onto State Route 77. When I leave Akron Road, I have to ease out onto that state highway for about three feet to see clearly to the north and see what is coming. Akron Road comes out onto Route 77 just above a hill that comes from the north, and so you sometimes can't see cars until they are coming over the top of that hill. Then there is the traffic to contend with coming from the south, where the Thruway is located, about a mile away, so there are a lot of cars and trucks to contend with. Now, it wouldn't be so bad if there weren't all those lilac bushes obstructing the view on the left side of Akron Road. They are never trimmed, and they are large ones that are blinding the view from the north. If the State Highway Dept. would take those bushes down, it would help the situation and it wouldn't be such a bad corner.

You know, life is like that with all its blind corners and weeds of sin. When we travel the roads of life, we need a road map to guide us, and thankfully we have the Bible, which safely takes us down those roads and around blind corners. God wants us to travel the roads of life with Him so that those blind corners of sin will not block our view of what God has in life for us. With God as my guide, I'll know how to navigate through those dangerous blind corners. Life's highway may not be all safe travel, but with God leading and guiding the way, I'll simply ignore the pitfalls of blind corners and travel wherever He takes me. In the Bible, in Psalm 32:8, it says, "I will instruct you and teach you in the way you should go: I will counsel you and watch over you."(NIV) Who better to travel with than God? I truly hope that you are traveling the roads of life with Him, as it's safer and smarter to rest in the care of the One who guides you and loves you the most. Guess I'll keep on traveling with the Lord right here at my kitchen table, and I won't worry about those blind corners, as God will safely lead me all the way if I trust in Him.

Letter #60

Fall Makes You Miss Mowing the Lawn

September 3, 2019

HOW DID AUGUST GO BY SO FAST, AND HOW DID September arrive so quickly? Summer seems to have rushed by before I realized what was going on. The last time I was sitting at my kitchen table to write to you was August 8, and here it is September 3, and August 2019 has come and gone. Is it just me or have those summer months disappeared a lot faster than usual? From June 21, when summer began, until now is like a blur, and starting September 21, we will be welcoming in that season of fall. As I get older, it seems that time goes faster than when I was younger. Also I realize that school is about to resume, and once again I ask, "Where did the summer go?"

Thankfully, I was busy with life, going to family reunions, and seeing old friends, so we didn't sit home and vegetate but kept busy. We have slowed down a little, but we still enjoy life, though at a slower pace. Richard is still mowing the church lawn (seven acres), and I decided that I should mow our lawn at home so he wouldn't have so much lawn to mow. I figured that I would be sitting and riding, with no walking, so it wouldn't be difficult for me to do. So far, I've enjoyed the time communing with nature and being alone with my thoughts for three hours, as that's how long it takes to mow the lawn. Now, when summer is gone, I won't have that work to do, and I'll miss it.

But I'm not going to worry about what the future brings; I'll take one day at a time and be thankful that God is in control, leading me in the ways I should go. In the Bible, in the Old Testament, in Jeremiah 29:11 it says, "'For I know the plans I have for you,' declares the Lord, 'plans to prosper you and not to harm you, plans to give you hope and a future.'"(NIV) It's nice to know that God has plans for us and we don't have to be concerned about the future. He didn't say we should sit and do nothing; He just doesn't want us to be worried about what is to come. I'm not going to be concerned that time goes by quickly, and I'm not going to worry about the seasons and what they might bring. I'll leave the future up to God and be thankful for each season of my life. I'll enjoy summer, fall, winter, and spring right here at my kitchen table and let God do all the planning.

Letter #61

Jesus Repairs Us No Matter How Tattered

October 8, 2019

WE'VE HAD A GREAT SUMMER, AND NOW THAT FALL is here and the days are getting shorter and darkness comes sooner, I will probably not be on the go so much. I don't like being out after dark, so I will most likely be reading more or watching TV instead. I also might be sitting at my kitchen table writing or enjoying my computer, where I love keeping in touch with those on Facebook. That includes relatives and friends who live out of state and out of the country as well as those who live close by.

The other day my great-niece Teri Silsby, from North Carolina, posted before and after pictures of a quilt that had been damaged by a dog. He had chewed the top of the quilt and ripped the middle and outside edges in many places. Teri repaired that quilt, and the finished product was beautiful. This was all done by hand-sewing, as she had to repair the top side as well as the underneath side and was unable to use a sewing machine. It took many hours of finding materials to match the different colors and then to cut each piece to fit and complete each block of that quilt. What a magnificent hand-repair job, and the finished product looked as good as new.

That was just a quilt, but that reminded me of what Jesus does for us. We ruin our lives with sins of all kinds, but when we go to Jesus and repent, He takes our tattered blanket of life and repairs it with His love and forgiveness. Those repairs make us as good as new. In 1 John 1:9 it says, "If we confess our sins, he is faithful and just and will forgive us our sins and cleanse us from all unrighteousness."(NIV) Jesus made that cleansing possible by shedding His blood on the cross, and no matter what those sins might be, He can repair the quilt of your life to look new again. I guess most of us like new things and new beginnings, so as fall comes and the weather changes, I'll just hunker down for the fall and winter months and enjoy life right here at my kitchen table.

Letter #62

Much to Be Thankful for This Year

November 12, 2019

It's November already. The time has changed from daylight saving time back to Eastern Standard Time, and we have had the first snow storm of the season, with about a foot of that fluffy white stuff covering the ground. Also, Thanksgiving is just around the corner. I guess you could say winter has arrived, even if the calendar doesn't say so.

For us this early part of November has been a very busy time. Our daughter Mona celebrated her seventieth birthday on November 7; it seems like only yesterday she was off to college. Now she was celebrating a milestone birthday, and I wanted to have a party for her with all the trimmings. Her sister Betty and sister-in-law Laurie provided the most perfect party with help from her brothers, Tracy and Ken, and sister-in-law, Jinner. Also several of the nieces and nephews and great-nieces and nephews helped host the birthday party. She received many cards and gifts from family and friends from far and near and will cherish those memories for days to come.

Now we are looking forward to that day of Thanksgiving when we stop to give thanks for all the many blessings we enjoy each and every day. If someone were to ask me what I was most thankful for, it would be hard to limit it to just one particular thing. But I do think that Jesus dying on the cross for me that I might have eternal life would be number one on my list. John 3:16 says, "For God so loved the world, that he gave his one and only Son, that whoever believes in Him shall not perish but have eternal life."(NIV)

Then there are so many other things I am thankful for that the list would go on and on. I think that living in the United States would be another one near the top of the list because of all the freedoms we have and the beautiful country where I live, as I would never want to live anywhere else but in western New York. I of course am most thankful for our four children and their spouses, our ten grandchildren and their spouses, and our twenty-six great-grandchildren—so I guess I could never stop thanking God for all the blessings that I have. Some things I take for granted, such as my eyesight, my hearing, a brain that can think, and the ability to talk. I've lost my sense of smell, which is bad enough, but I can still be thankful for what I do have. In 1 Thessalonians 5:16–18 it says, "Be joyful always; pray continually; give thanks in all circumstances, for this is God's will for you in Christ Jesus."(NIV)

Now, that is good advice: to be joyful, pray, and give thanks. So this Thanksgiving I plan on doing just that, and what better place to give thanks than right here at my kitchen table.

Letter #63
Thank the Lord for His Blessings
November 26, 2019

I KNOW THIS IS ANOTHER LETTER MUCH SOONER than usual, but the last letter Paul Trowbridge wrote was such a great read that I wanted to comment on how much I enjoyed what he stated in his letter. Paul told how much he and his wife enjoy being farmers and how fulfilling their lives are. He and his wife had just finished putting fresh straw bedding down before letting the animals into the barn, and as Paul sat on a bale of straw, he watched them as they entered. The joy he felt while observing his animals and the gratitude and appreciation that his animals showed for the clean straw was a sight to behold. Paul watched as the animals jumped for joy and pranced about, snuggling down into the straw bedding; he was amazed at their reaction. What a picture Paul painted with his words.

All this got me to thinking, do I jump for joy or give thanks for all the "fresh, clean straws of blessings" that God provides for me each day? Do I give a second thought to the many things God gives me that I take for granted, such as the air that I breathe, the sunrises and the sunsets, the birds chirping in the early morning hours, the sight of a green tree that turns to bright yellow, and the fluttering of its leaves as they fall to the ground? And how about the beauty of the first snowfall, as it blankets the earth and turns it into a wonderland of pristine beauty? Do I snuggle down into the beauty of another day without so much as a prayer of thanks?

I think God had a great time when He created the earth and all the wonderful things for us to enjoy, and if you read Genesis chapter one, you will know what I mean. After each day that He created something, God saw "that it was good" (Gen. 1:9,12,18,20,25, and 31; NIV). So at this time of the year, let's be like those animals and prance, jump, and snuggle into the love of God to show how very much we are thankful for. Let God and those family members and friends know how very much we love and appreciate them and life itself. Psalm 100:1–3 says, "Shout for joy to the Lord, all the earth, Worship the Lord with gladness come before Him with joyful songs. Know that the Lord is God. It is He who made us, and we are his: we are his people, the sheep of his pasture."(NIV)

Now, I think that is almost like what the animals did, except for the shouting. We can't all sit with Paul on that bale of straw, but we can shout for joy and praise God no matter where we are sitting. So on Thanksgiving Day, I'll be at my kitchen table, and wherever you are sitting, let us all be thankful together.

Letter #64

Sharing Christmas Wishes and Memories

December 9, 2019

"MERRY CHRISTMAS." GUESS THAT IS NOT POLITI-cally correct to some of you, but it is to me. Christmas is the celebration of Christ's birthday, and Christmas starts with the word *Christ*, so it must be OK to say, "Merry Christmas." In Luke 2:7 it says, "And she brought forth her first born son, and wrapped Him in swaddling clothes, and laid Him in a manger; because there was no room for them in the inn."(KJV) And I'm so thankful that we can celebrate His birthday. Yes, it's almost Christmas; no, it's Christmas every day when we have Jesus in our heart.

Here in my house it really looks like Christmas, as my daughter Mona came over Monday and Tuesday and decorated four areas of our home with festive Christmas decorations. Yes, it takes her two days or more to complete the task.

For years I've been collecting nativity sets in all shapes and sizes. There are large sets, small ones, miniature ones, and even ones on blankets, pillows, music boxes, and tablecloths. If it's a nativity/manger scene, I have it. I really don't know how many I own but probably close to a hundred. Now Mona doesn't display all of them, as there is not enough room, but she does a great job and gives the house a very Christmassy look.

There are also other decorations associated with Christmas that are not spiritual but are on the worldly side that I collect. But in case you need some help in guessing, it's that little, red-nosed reindeer that has the same last name as I do—Rudolph, of course! He also comes in all sizes, shapes, and forms, such as plush, cuddly ones; wooden ones; and yes, on blankets, pillows, quilts, cups, and men's caps, and also deer horns and a red nose for our car. I also have a few figures of Santa, music boxes, candles, and angels. Mona also puts up two Christmas trees, one in the living room and one in the blue family room. Now, if you have a few minutes, let me tell you why it takes so long to put up all those decorations.

In the living room, she puts up a small Christmas tree with different colored lights, garland, and ornaments. One large nativity set with seventeen figurines of Mary, Joseph, Jesus, angels, shepherds, wise men, camels, and lambs are displayed on top of the TV cabinet. This was a gift I received some forty-two years ago from my neighbor Pam Neuroth in appreciation for taking her family of five into our home during the blizzard of 1977. Other decorations include thirty other nativity sets, music boxes, a lighted plastic church, bells, holly, red poinsettia flowers, candles, and gold beads nestled among the decorations.

The dining room area is all in silver and blue, with angels, snowmen, glass nativity globes, a blue nativity set, blue candle decorations, music boxes, silver beads, and white, fluffy cotton that looks like snow piled around the silvery items.

The kitchen area shelves are lined with white, and my miniature pewter Hallmark nativity set is there. The set includes shepherds, wise men, and the manger scene, with Mary, Joseph, and baby Jesus, and was given to me by my sister-in-law, Lois. I treasure this set, as Lois is no longer with us. Also on these shelves are seven small nativity sets, candles, Christmas mice, and cute decorated deer. I also have a live red poinsettia on the counter by the sink, an early Christmas gift from my granddaughter Debbie, as well as four nativity sets.

Next comes the blue family room, and that is where the Rudolphs are displayed. The blankets, pillows, small rug, stuffed huggable plush ones, and music-playing Rudolphs are everywhere—on the window seat and the backs of sofas and chairs, and a wooden window box nativity set hangs on the wall overlooking the room. Also two white plush teddy bears from the Christmas of 2002 and other stuffed toys are arranged on one side of the steps, with Rudolph wreaths hanging on the door. And there on the south wall is the large tree, which is loaded with ornaments, white lights, and garland, lighting up the room with its sparkling lights and glitter.

The decorating is all finished, the house is aglow, and I realize there is something missing: preparing my heart for Christmas. Yes, the decorations are nice, but my heart is more important to God. He needs to know that I too am ready for Christmas. It's not the buying of gifts and the decorations that make Christmas; it's the gift of Jesus, born thousands of years ago He is no longer in that manger where the shepherds came and worshipped Him. He is right here with us. But you have to be the one to let Him into your heart. Romans 10:10 says, "For it is with your heart that you believe and are justified, and it is with your mouth that you confess and are saved."(NIV) Why not let this Christmas be the best

Christmas you've ever had and accept God's Christmas gift? And from me to all of you, let me say "Merry Christmas" from my decorated kitchen table.

Letter #65

Reflecting on 2019, Looking to 2020

December 28, 2019

JUST GOT HOME FROM CELEBRATING CHRISTMAS with the Klotzbach side of the family, and I'm walking on air, as I had a great time. It's great getting together and sharing memories and having another Christmas with the family.

There are only four of us left from the original family of Peter Klotzbach Jr.: Eleanor, Kathryn, Ellen, and I. Unfortunately, Eleanor was not able to come because of health reasons, and my youngest sister, Ellen, lives in Arizona and couldn't make it this year. So, Kathryn and I were the only two there of the original thirteen children. My husband, Richard, sister-in-law Jeanne, and brother-in-law Roger were also able to be there, as well as many of the grandchildren and great-grandchildren and a few great-great-grandchildren, which made for an enjoyable gathering. We still enjoy seeing each other and remembering past days, so we decided that we would plan next year's Christmas party early. We'll leave it on the fourth Saturday of December, at the same time and same place, to carry on the family tradition of getting together for Christmas.

Then I remembered that in three short days this year of 2019 will be a year of the past, and we will be welcoming in another New Year. How did this past year fly by so quickly? Maybe it's because we've been so blessed and had a great year, with some ups and a few downs but still healthy and able to enjoy life.

Have you made plans for this coming year of 2020, or do you plan on taking one day at a time? In the Bible, in Jeremiah 29:11–12, it says, "'I know the plans I have for you,' says the Lord; 'plans to prosper you and not to harm you, plans to give you hope and a future. Then you will call upon me and come and pray to me, and I will listen to you.'"(NIV) God will lead if you go to Him in prayer and rely on what plans He has for you. Guess I won't make any New Year's resolutions, as I will relax, pray, and see what God has planned for me right here at my kitchen table.

Letter #66
Recalling the Blizzard of '77

January 29, 2020

GOT OUT OF BED EARLY, WENT TO THE WINDOW TO look out and greet God, thanking Him for waking me. Sometimes we forget to thank Him for the little joys of life, such as getting out of bed and being able to walk, think, and take nourishment. But today I paused for a long time at the window, looking at the wintry scene that God gave to me; the white blanket of snow that covered the ground, the frosty trees that sparkled like diamonds, and the glow of the sunlight from the east all made for a perfect picture of winter. How fortunate I am to be in a warm, toasty home enjoying the morning scene of winter from my kitchen table.

January has almost lived out its days, and I realize that it's quiet outside, no winter storm like we had several years ago when that blizzard of '77 hit with a vengeance. I was at work at Akron School, and there was no storm in sight. We had been warned that a bad storm was coming, and our district superintendent had called off school for the children, but we office workers had to go anyway. It was about 10:30 when it started to snow just a little. It was hard to keep my mind on the office work as I kept looking out and wanting to go home. I got a call from my daughter Mona at about 1:00 p.m. Mona worked nights at Genesee Memorial Hospital but awoke early and, seeing the weather conditions, called and suggested that I better get home soon, as the weather was getting worse and it was getting hard to see. Finally, at 3:30 p.m. Dr. Fish let us leave. I called my daughter Betty at her place of work and asked if she wanted me to come get her, but her boss wouldn't let her go. He was sure it would end soon. So I started home, which was only three miles away, but the roads were hard to get through and the visibility was really bad. I got to the five corners and barely made it through the intersection and had another two miles to go. I hit snowdrift after snowdrift until I reached home. My 1976 Chevy barreled through our snow-filled driveway and finally made it into the garage. I was shaking and scared but safe at home.

That storm went on for days and the wind never stopped blowing, but the worst was yet to come. My husband, Richard, was the superintendent of highways during that blizzard, and he never stopped working. Keeping the roads open was almost impossible, and doing the emergency things kept him and his men busy throughout the week of that storm.

My son Ken was married, and he and his wife lived in Maryland. I wrote letters to him every day about that blizzard. It was like a journal, as there was no mail for several days, so I just kept adding another page to the letter. I still have that journal of the blizzard and what happened for those few days. It's much too long to tell in this letter, but I ended up with a full house, as our neighbor down the road—a family of five—didn't have heat in their home, so they came here to stay. My son Tracy was still living at home, as he was still in high school. My daughter Betty finally got here by snowmobile a day later from her job in Akron. Her husband, David "Boots," managed to get here from where he had been snowed in at his job, but no Richard, as he was busy with the storm that just wouldn't stop. I didn't see him until the storm ended several days later.

The pipes from our house into the septic tank were frozen, so I hung a five-gallon bucket on the outlet pipe and caught all the water and waste from the toilets and sinks. With so many people here, I had to empty that pail into the farmer's field across the road. With the wind, zero visibility, and freezing cold, it was an unpleasant and cold task to perform.

But we had electricity, food, heat, and a telephone, and we were safe, so we praised God for His love and care. Psalm 68:19 says, "Praise be to the Lord, to God our Savior, who daily bears our burdens."(NIV) Yes, God kept us all safe during that storm, and He is still loving us and keeping us warm this winter. It's always fun to reminisce about past winters and to be thankful for God's love and care. Also, that we live in America, where we have all the many conveniences we take for granted. I'll enjoy the next two months of winter and keep looking and watching for those little signs of spring outside my kitchen window, right here at my kitchen table.

Letter #67

True Love Should Not Just Be a Valentine's Day Celebration

February 14, 2020

GOT UP A LITTLE LATER THAN USUAL, AND AS I entered the dining room, my eyes caught sight of something on the kitchen table. A large red box shaped like a heart, with a card on the top, was at my place. I slid into my chair and opened the card and smiled as I read that special valentine card from my husband, Richard. After I'd gone to bed, he must have put that box of candy and card for me to find in the morning. My eyes filled with tears of joy as I read those special words on the card and thought about the first time he gave me a box of candy in a heart-shaped box seventy-two years ago. Funny how memories can return to fill your thoughts and recall past years to reminisce about.

Seventy-two years ago when we were dating, Richard brought me a heart-shaped box of chocolates similar to this one, and I remember feeling so special, as I'd never had a gift like that before. Remembering brought a smile to my face, and

I treasured the thought of that day so many years ago. Now, years later we are still thankful for the love we have shared all these years.

Thinking how special Valentine's Day has become and how much money is spent on flowers, candies, cards, jewelry, and other gifts is amazing. It's hard to believe that only one day is set aside to show the love we feel for others. Maybe if we would let each day of the year glow with love for one another, there wouldn't be time to argue, disagree, fight, and hate.

This reminds me of a Scripture found in Luke 10:27, which says, "Love the Lord your God with all your heart and with all your soul and with all your strength, and with all your mind, and love your neighbor as yourself."(NIV) Now, if we all did that, we would have 365 days to celebrate love all year long, not just on Valentine's Day.

Another verse for all of us to remember is found in Romans 5:8, which says, "But God demonstrates his own love for us in this: While we were still sinners, Christ died for us." (NIV) Maybe we are looking for love in all the wrong places when it's right in front of us. My hope for each of you is that you find that special love of God, of loved ones and friends, to enjoy every day.

In the meantime, I'll keep sending my letters to the editor for all of you to enjoy. With love and hugs from my kitchen table.

Letter #68

We Must All Work Together Against Corona Virus

March 20, 2020

A LOT HAS HAPPENED SINCE I LAST WROTE MY Valentine's Day message, and life has changed for all of us. This coronavirus has made a great difference in all of our lives, and the canceling of events and other issues have changed the way we live each day. Don't get me wrong, I know this canceling of every event in our lives is much needed, as that virus is a dangerous illness, and we need to take precautions.

My husband, Richard, turns ninety-five on March 23, and we had planned an open-house party on Sunday, March 22, to celebrate that event. When we learned that all events and gatherings of more than ten people would not be allowed, we knew we would have to cancel that party, so we did. Also our Indian Falls Methodist Church was involved in the Maple Weekend, where we sell breakfast and lunch at the Maple Moons Farm for two of the weekends, and all the profits go to Feed the Hungry; now that has been canceled too. Schools have been called off for an indefinite length of time, making it hard for those who still have to work to arrange for childcare. They have asked that the elderly remain at home if possible and let others shop for them.

The disruption to all our lives is taking a toll on the entire world, and our leaders are doing their best to take control of every aspect of this situation and do what is best for all of us. So I am grateful for President Trump, all the world leaders, doctors and nurses, and others who are taking control of the situation and providing us with protection and helping us deal with the scarcity of food, water, toilet paper, and other necessities that we take for granted.

I don't think we need to be afraid or worried, as that would not be a healthy thing to do. We must have trust and most of all hope that the end of this will be soon if we work together. Not judging or blaming others but working with them. Let us remember that "we are one nation under God," and He is our hope and our trust. In Isaiah 40: 31 it says, "But those who hope in the Lord will renew their strength. They will soar on wings like eagles; they will run and not grow weary, they will walk and not be faint."(NIV) If we have this hope and trust in the Lord our God to see us through this pandemic, we will survive.

So as long as we have to stay home, I'll be praying for all of you and for our country and those in authority, and someday soon America will be back to normal. In the meantime, I'll sit at my kitchen table, where I can eat, watch TV, read, have prayer time and meditation, and enjoy my second cup of coffee.

Letter #69

Even without Going to Church, We Can Celebrate Easter

April 6, 2020

IT'S THE DAY AFTER PALM SUNDAY AND THE FOURTH Sunday we've had to miss attending church. It really doesn't seem like a Sunday when you are used to going no matter what the weather or how tired you are. Going to church is the normal thing for me to do. Now since this "stay at home" came into being, I'm confined at my kitchen table, able to look out my window but not able to go to church and be with others, and it looks like we will still be quarantined for Easter Sunday.

But that doesn't mean I can't celebrate Easter. I will celebrate that empty tomb, Jesus rising from the dead, His resurrection, and the fact that Jesus is alive today in my heart and in the hearts of many other Christians all over the world. The coronavirus may have stopped the whole world, caused fear and death, and paralyzed our economy, but it hasn't stopped the spread of God's Word.

This week is what has been known as Holy Week, where we as Christians relive that last week before Jesus' death. It starts with Jesus' triumphant entry into Jerusalem riding on a donkey, where He is praised and honored as their king, spreading palm branches and their cloaks on the ground before Him while shouting "Hosanna in the highest" as He passes by. You can read all about this in the Bible, in Mark 11:1–11 (NIV).

For Jesus, this week proves to be a busy one and also the end of His physical life. Holy Week, which started with such promise and excitement, ended at Calvary with the crucifixion of Jesus. Each day from Monday until Wednesday are great days for Jesus as He chases the moneychangers out of the temple and then preaches and teaches in the temple with the Sadducees and Pharisees watching, hoping to get a chance to have Him arrested or even to kill him. Read Mark 11:15–19.

Thursday is the start of Passover and the Feast of Unleavened Bread, special Holy Days for Jesus and the disciples to celebrate. Read Mark 14:12–16. While having supper, Jesus informs them that one of them will betray Him. Jesus serves them their first communion, breaking the bread representing His body and serving the cup of wine representing His blood, shed for us all. After supper they sing hymns and leave the room and go out to the Mount of Olives. Read Mark 14:17–26. Thursday night Jesus prays alone in the Garden of Gethsemane as His disciples sleep. Then early Friday, before dawn, Jesus is arrested. Read Mark 14:32–46.

Jesus is first taken to the religious leaders, the Sanhedrin, where He is put on trial on trumped-up charges and found guilty. During this time Peter denies Jesus three times and the rooster crows. Read Mark 14:55–72.

Very early on Friday morning the Sanhedrin bind Jesus and hand Him over to Pilate. Once again Jesus is on trial but doesn't defend himself. Pilate finds no fault in Jesus, but because the crowd is in a frenzy and cry, "Crucify Jesus!" Pilate releases Barabbas and sentences Jesus to death. First he has Jesus flogged. Read Mark 15:1–15.

The soldiers lead Jesus away. They mock Him by putting a purple robe on Him and a crown of thorns on His head. They hail Jesus as King of the Jews. They spit on him, strike Him on the head, and fall on their knees before Him and mock him. Then putting on His own clothes, they lead Him away to be crucified. Jesus is weak, hungry, bleeding, and thirsty as He struggles to walk, bearing the weight of the cross on His shoulders. Read Mark 15:16–20.

On a hill called Golgotha, there Jesus is nailed to that cross, and two thieves, one on either side, are crucified with him. It's about the third hour of the day (9:00 in the morning). A sign above Jesus's head reads KING OF THE JEWS. One of the thieves accepts Jesus as Lord; the other one mocks Jesus and asks Him to save them all if He is the king. Read Mark 15:25–32.

At the sixth hour (12:00 noon), darkness covers the earth until the ninth hour, which is 3:00 p.m., when Jesus finally cries out in a loud voice, "My God, my God, why have you forsaken me?" and with a loud cry, Jesus breathes His last. Read Mark 15:33–37.

The hour is late when Joseph of Arimathea asks Pilate for Jesus' body. He hurries, as the Jewish Sabbath begins at sunset. He lays Jesus in a borrowed tomb, wrapped in spices and grave cloths. A large stone is rolled against the entrance. Read Mark 15:42–46

On Saturday, which was the Jewish Sabbath, nothing was mentioned. But early on our Sunday, which would have been their first day of the week, the women brought spices to anoint Jesus' body. They didn't know how they would roll the stone away, but when they got there, the stone was gone and so was Jesus' body. A man in white told them that Jesus had risen and to go tell His disciples, but they were afraid and didn't. Jesus first appeared to Mary Magdalene, and she ran and told the disciples that Jesus was alive. Read Mark 16:1–14.

Yes, Jesus was resurrected, and He still lives today. We can't see Him physically, but we can feel Him spiritually in our hearts. He sent the Holy Spirit to be with us, and when we accept Jesus into our hearts, the Holy Spirit is with us forever. Even if we can't attend church, we can still celebrate Easter wherever we are, even at my kitchen table.

Letter #70

Life Comes with Many Puzzle Pieces

April 16, 2020

WELL, WE ARE STILL QUARANTINED AND NOT allowed to visit other people except by phone, email, or Facebook. I'm fortunate that I have my husband, Richard, to talk with and fix meals for, so I'm not lonely. We are doing very well and are so thankful that we are not sick. We do watch a lot of TV and go on Facebook quite a bit, and I keep busy fixing meals and doing the word puzzles in the *Daily News*. I've heard that some have been busy cleaning drawers, sending cards, putting pictures into albums, and doing puzzles; I've only done a few small puzzles of one hundred pieces but nothing big. Actually puzzles are a fascinating project if you want something to do.

Years ago I read an article about an eighty-six-year-old man, Jack Harris, who spent seven long years putting a five-thousand-piece puzzle together only to discover that the last piece was missing. He was so devastated and couldn't find a replacement, as that particular puzzle was out of print. The picture was of a painting by French artist James Tissot and was done in

1862. Now a British Newspaper, the *Sun*, had commissioned a perfect copy of the lost piece to be made, and when it was put into place, photographers were there to record the occasion. As I read about this, I began to have the thought that our lives are like a puzzle.

That puzzle was of the Prodigal Son from the Bible (Luke 15:11–24), who thought that when he left his father's home, his life was finally all together. He had what he wanted—money from his father, the ability to be on his own; the pieces of his life's puzzle were all in place, only to realize several months later that his puzzle had fallen apart and all he had left were broken pieces. Then he remembered his father had servants, and just maybe he could be a servant; at least he would have food to eat and a place to stay. So he picked up those dirty pieces of the puzzle of his life and went home. When his father ran to meet him and embrace him, the puzzle of his life finally came together. The big piece that was missing was his father's love.

Like that son, we didn't listen to our Heavenly Father, so He sent us Jesus to be the missing piece. No puzzle is complete without all the pieces, and if one is missing, it will spoil the whole picture. In John 14:6 Jesus said, "I am the way, the truth, and the life: No one comes to the Father, except through me."(NIV) So you see, Jesus is that missing piece; he fills that space in our puzzle. Yes, Jesus is the "special piece," and some people never find it or wait too long and grow old still searching for the lost puzzle piece. If we put that lost piece of Jesus into our heart and make Jesus the centerpiece and also the central peace of the puzzle of life, then our life's puzzle will be complete. I'm so happy that I found that missing piece to my life's puzzle and that by living for Jesus my picture is complete with no pieces missing. Guess I'll sit right here at my kitchen table and relax by putting a puzzle together.

Letter #71

Remembering Mary, Mother of Jesus, as Mother's Day Approaches

May 5, 2020

ACCORDING TO THE CALENDAR, IT'S ALMOST Mother's Day, and I'm realizing that I have been a mother for more than seventy years. I became a mom when I was nineteen, and it's been the best and most fulfilling profession anyone could ever have been blessed with. Mothering sort of becomes second nature to a woman no matter what age she might be; it seems to be born into her. Since that first time of becoming a mother to my daughter Mona, I have been blessed by becoming a mother to three others—my son Kenneth, my daughter Betty, and my son Tracy.

Now, don't get me wrong: being a mother is not all peaches and cream; there are days you are so tired that you just want to quit, and then there are days that keep you on a high and give you the courage you need to go on. The ups and downs and all that is in between has been a rollercoaster ride, and I'm grateful that I had Jesus along as a helper and guide. Psalm 121:2 says,

"MY help comes from the Lord, the Maker of heaven and earth." (NIV) Yes, it surely does.

I've been thinking about one of the most famous and most special moms who ever lived, and that was Mary, the mother of Jesus; she was only a teenager at the time. Only a lowly virgin peasant girl pledged to a man named Joseph. Thinking about her life gave me cause to give her honor on this Mother's Day. She lived in disgrace, as she was pregnant with God's child but couldn't tell anyone. Mary had to travel ninety miles, being very pregnant, and give birth to the King of Kings in a smelly stable, with only her husband, Joseph, and the animals present. Then shepherds came, and when they left, Mary was in awe and could only ponder all this in her heart.

We don't hear much of His mother, Mary, until she travels with Jesus at the age of twelve to visit the temple in Jerusalem. On their way home, Mary and Joseph discover that Jesus is not with them. Anxiously they hurry back to Jerusalem, which takes them three days, before they find their young Son. He is at the temple listening to the teachers and asking questions. Of course Mary is upset, as that's how any mother would feel. In Luke 2:48b–49, she scolds Jesus and says, "Son, why have you treated us like this? Your father and I have anxiously been searching for you." Jesus says, "Why were you searching for me? Didn't you know I had to be in my Father's House?"(NIV) We don't know if Mary understood this, but it may have been one more thing she pondered in her heart. Nothing more of Jesus' childhood is recorded in the Bible.

Then the next time we hear of Mary is at the wedding feast where she asks Jesus to turn water into wine, as they had run out. This is the beginning of Jesus' ministry, and He is now thirty years old. His ministry will last for only three short years, and during this time, we hear little about His mother, Mary.

What we do know is that Mary was there when her Son was crucified. The tears she must have shed were those of a mother who loved Him and didn't understand why Jesus gave up His life for all of us.

Then three days later, Mary finds out her Son is alive; He has risen from the dead and walks and talks with His disciples. I don't know how Mary felt when she heard that Jesus was alive, but thinking as a mother, it had to be a moment of hope and unbelievable happiness. I'm thankful that Mary was Jesus' mother; she was only a teenager, but she did what God asked her to do. We too can be like Mary, and when God asks us to do His will, we can say yes and let Him lead the way.

My wish for all of you is to have a great Mother's Day, whether you are a mother, stepmother, aunt, niece, sister, grandmother, or little girl. Enjoy being you, and I can do that too, right here at my kitchen table.

Letter #72

Memorial Day Remains–
Even When Quarantined

May 22, 2020

WELL, THIS IS THE BEGINNING OF A THREE-DAY holiday, and we can't even celebrate it like we used to, as we are still quarantined. Yes, this is Memorial Day weekend, when we remember those veterans and others who gave their lives so that we can have freedom to live in America and be governed by the people and for the people.

Today my husband, Richard, will place American flags on the graves of all the veterans buried in the Indian Falls Cemetery. It's always been a task that he has felt privileged to perform. Those flags are a symbol of our country, and they are a way to let others know those veterans buried there are appreciated. A reminder that they were in the service to protect America and those they loved so that we can have those freedoms we enjoy here in America.

Memorial celebrations were first started back in 1865 by freed slaves who honored graves of Union soldiers buried in

South Carolina by placing flowers on their graves. The official celebration was begun after the Civil War in 1868 by the Grand Army of the Republic (GAR) and was officially called Decoration Day. If you enjoy history, go on your computer and Google "Decoration Day," and there you will find the whole story of how it began.

I looked up the meaning of *Memorial* in the dictionary, and the number-one meaning is "something designed to keep remembrance alive." Yes, that is what Memorial Day is all about—honoring those men and women who have died in wars and remembering their sacrifice. A way of thanking them for giving their lives so that we can have the freedoms we enjoy today.

There is another One who also gave His life by dying on a cross two thousand years ago so that we can be free from sin and have a life with Him in heaven, and that is Jesus, God's only Son. Jesus has asked us that when we take communion, to remember Him. In Luke 22:19–20 it says, "And he took bread, gave thanks, and broke it, and gave it to them, saying, 'This is my body given for you; do this in remembrance of me.' In the same way, after the supper He took the cup, saying, 'This cup is the new covenant in my blood, which is poured out for you.'"(NIV) So let us remember the sacrifice Jesus made when He died on that cross so that we can have life with Him in eternity, and also remember those veterans who gave their lives for us. And even though I'm still in quarantine, I can do that right here at my kitchen table.

Letter #73

Corona Virus Can't Stop Us from Honoring Our Fathers

June 4, 2020

TODAY THE SUN IS SHINING WITH A SLIGHT BREEZE, and the temperature is already 74 degrees. The last few days have been rainy and a little on the cool side, so this is a welcome relief. When June comes it seems that we can relax and know that summer is here. Looking at the calendar, it won't be officially summer until June 20, but I'm going to say it is, because it's the month of June.

Yes, the month of June seems to shout, "I'm a great month, so it's time to celebrate!" It's the month of so many special events. It's a wonderful month to have a wedding, to celebrate graduations, and of course a time to celebrate fathers. Now, because of the coronavirus, these kinds of celebrations are all being canceled or put on hold. It's a real shame those kids who have worked and studied hard and completed thirteen years of schooling aren't allowed to march down the aisle to receive their high school diplomas. What a heart break for those couples who have dreamed of, planned, and waited for their special wedding day only to have it canceled or shortened to a small family reception. When it comes to Father's Day, I don't think they can stop us from celebrating fathers on that special day. We don't need permission to love our dads; we can show our love and respect every day of the year.

My father is no longer with me, but I can still remember those precious times we shared. The love he gave, the prayers he prayed for me, and his knowledge and understanding of life and spiritual matters will always remain in my heart and thoughts. My heart goes out to those of you who were not blessed as I with such a loving father.

My earthly father may be gone, but I have a really great Heavenly Father, who loves me and speaks to me every day through His Word. God wants more than anything to be your Father too. The only way to God is to accept Jesus into your heart and live for Him. John 14:6 says, "I am the way the truth and the life. No one comes to the Father except through me."(NIV) Years ago I asked Jesus to come into my heart, and when I did, God became my Heavenly Father.

You too can have God as your Father, by accepting Jesus into your heart. In 2 Corinthians 6:18 it says, "I will be a Father to you, and you will be my sons and daughters, says the Lord Almighty."(NIV) This proves that God wants to be your Heavenly Father, but it's all up to you to make that choice.

Now, let me wish all fathers everywhere a happy Father's Day, and I can do that right here from my kitchen table.

Letter #74
Work, a Gift from God

August 20, 2020

Hi, everybody. I haven't written in so long, you most likely have forgotten that I write these letters to the editor. My last one was in June, and I didn't even write one for the month of July. I missed a very important date, Independence Day, or better known as the Fourth of July, a special time to celebrate the birth of our great nation and the signing of the Declaration of Independence. We missed all the parades and Akron fireworks but did enjoy many fireworks from our kitchen window and our living room window. This time of being quarantined, my husband and I have been fortunate to have each other and not be alone like so many of our friends. So thankful to God for allowing us to be alive, able to get around and be in our home, get meals and go for groceries, and also to be able to enjoy a meal out at our local Candy Apple restaurant in Akron. I'm happy that things are getting back to "sort of normal."

Richard does keep busy doing jobs outside and keeping the lawn mowed. Of course he does some jobs that I think no man of ninety-five years of age should be doing, such as trimming the nine trees in our yard with his large tree trimmers, and he did it all in one afternoon. Then he was too tired to pick up all the branches, so he waited until the next day and asked three of our great-grandsons—Mavrik, 13; Stetson, 11; and MacKoy, 10—to come and pick them up. The branches filled his pickup truck to overflowing, so he was grateful for the boys' help. I, of course, sputtered that he shouldn't be doing jobs like that anymore, and he told me that as long as he could still walk and get around, he was going to keep busy. In Ecclesiastes 5:18–19 it says, "Then I realized that it is good and proper for a man to eat and drink, and to find satisfaction in his toilsome labor under the sun during the few days of life God has given him—for this is his lot. Moreover, when God gives any man wealth and possessions, and enables him to enjoy them, to accept his lot and be happy in his work—this is a gift of God."(NIV)

Yes, those two verses convinced me that work is a gift from God, and we should be happy that we have work to keep us busy, no matter how old we are. So I'll stop sputtering and leave it all up to God to keep Richard safe, and I can do that right here at my kitchen table.

About the Author

I WAS BORN ON OCTOBER 14, 1930, IN A BIG OL' farmhouse on a three-hundred-acre farm in western New York, to Clara and Peter Klotzbach Jr. Ours was a close-knit family of thirteen children—six boys and seven girls—and I am the tenth child in line. I learned about the love of Jesus as a young child and accepted Jesus into my heart at the age of twelve, and through the years I have grown in my faith.

I married my husband, Richard Rudolph, on October 22, 1948, in our newly built Methodist church, in Indian Falls, New York. Ours was the second wedding in that new church building. This past October we celebrated our seventy-second anniversary, and during those past years our family has grown from a family of two to a family of fifty-six.

Each day after breakfast, Richard and I have family devotions and prayer time, where we pray for each of the fifty-six members of our family, for friends and neighbors, and for others we know who need prayer. It's a great way to start the day.

I am thankful to God for His grace and for my faith and ability to witness to others of Jesus' love, right here at my kitchen table.

49 of our 56 member Rudolph Family, October 2018

CPSIA information can be obtained
at www.ICGtesting.com
Printed in the USA
LVHW071143310721
694127LV00010BA/282